the

early jewish community

of

boston's north end

BY ARNOLD A. WIEDER

A SOCIOLOGICALLY ORIENTED STUDY OF AN
EASTERN EUROPEAN JEWISH IMMIGRANT
COMMUNITY IN AN AMERICAN BIG-CITY
NEIGHBORHOOD BETWEEN 1870 AND 1900

WITH AN INTRODUCTION BY JEROME HIMELHOCH

BRANDEIS UNIVERSITY 1962

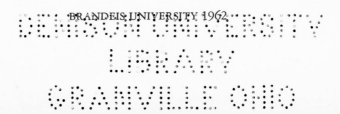

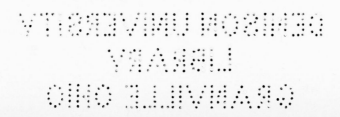

acknowledgements

THE RESEARCH PROJECT which led to the writing of this book was conducted under the provisions of a grant to Brandeis University by the Ethel Bresloff Fund, of which Colonel Bernard L. Gorfinkle of Boston is the executor.

It was the wish of the late Miss Bresloff, herself originally from the North End, to have the memory of her native community perpetuated through literary means. It was left to Col. Gorfinkle, also a distinguished former North Ender, to accomplish this aim.

When the book was written, another respected former resident of this neighborhood, the late Miss Fanny Goldstein, former Curator of Judaica at the Boston Public Library, conducted an extensive search for the fine old photographs included in this volume. In addition, the author is grateful for her comments on the text.

In the scholastic sense, the writer is deeply indebted to Professor Jerome Himelhoch who guided the study from its inception and provided invaluable advice during many conferences; to Dr. Abram L. Sachar, president of Brandeis University, who originally outlined

5

the project, and Professors Abraham G. Duker, Hyman B. Grinstein, Oscar Handlin and Isidore S. Meyer, each of whom shared his time with the author. Col. Gorfinkle helped in many ways, especially by making contact with prospective interviewees. He followed the project with close attention throughout. Dr. Benjamin Halpern, then of Harvard University, now Associate Professor of Near Eastern Studies at Brandeis University, read the typescript and made many very valuable suggestions. Mr. Harry Dubinsky contributed many insights and valuable materials.

The typing was expertly done by Mrs. James Zung.

Mr. Henry Selib, who was in charge of publication on behalf of the University, helped solve the many problems connected with the final preparations for printing and with seeing the book through the press.

The writer also wishes to thank Dean Eisig Silberschlag of the Hebrew Teachers College, Brookline, Mass., for permission to complete this work while serving as a member of his faculty.

Above all, everyone concerned with the project is grateful to the many men and women who shared their memories with us. We trust it will please them to find within these pages what we learned from them.

table of contents

introduction

RABBI WIEDER'S fascinating history of the early Jewish community of the North End of Boston will appeal to several groups of readers. To the layman he tells a lively story of immigrants escaping from the *shtetl** of Eastern Europe to create a new Jewish and American way of life in the streets of Boston. To the social historian it is the account of the migration of one ethnic group to a Boston neighborhood during the last three decades of the nineteenth century and at the same time it is part of the larger epic of the great Atlantic migration of Europeans to the New World. This monograph also contains material of sociological, anthropological, and economic interest. The author discusses, among other things, intergroup contacts, acculturation, value conflict, social change, family structure, the economics of peddling, and the sociology of religion. These phenomena and their interrelations are presented in five chapters: Immigration, Making a Living, Homes and Family Life, Religious Life, and Raising a New Generation.

Wieder's major contribution, as I see it, is to challenge the traditional view of sociologists and historians

*A glossary of Yiddish and Hebrew expressions will be found on page 79. With few exceptions, Eastern European colloquial forms and pronunciation were followed in transcription.

concerning the relation between the foreign-born first and the native-born second generations. In the traditional view, the fathers cling tenaciously to the Old World culture, while the sons bitterly rebel against their parents and their heritage. Wieder's evidence points to a different conclusion. He finds that the rapid acculturation of the second generation was of the making of the fathers — a direct result of the attitudinal changes of the first generation. The "revolt" of the second generation was only an overt manifestation of the unacknowledged wishes of the first. Behind their external traditionalism the parents often condoned and perhaps subtly encouraged their children's lapses from orthodoxy. (Conformist parents, according to some psychologists, sometimes unwittingly encourage their children to act out the parents' own non-conformist phantasies.) Inasmuch as many of the parents felt that a synthesis of Judaism and Americanism was impossible, they decided on the former for themselves and on the latter for their children.

The author further enhances our understanding of immigrant adjustment by tracing the unanticipated consequences of American freedom and economic opportunity. The father's dedication to his arduous job, which devoured him from the end of one sabbath until the beginning of the next, turned education, religion, and child-rearing over to the mother and changed the authority structure of the family. Although the result was again unforeseen, the economic and prestige value of secular education diverted the traditional Jewish devotion to learning from religious channels. Secular educational achievement, in turn, led to economic advancement, assimilation, and a rather extensive abandonment of dogma and ritual.

Another useful observation of the author is his suggestion that more attention should be given to the small pilot community which precedes the formation of the large ethnic colony in an urban area. The early Jewish North Enders, dispersed among the Yankees and Irish, assimilated faster than the later arrivals. When the "greenhorns" came, they looked up to the veteran settlers as leaders, teachers, landlords, and employers. By transmitting their own blend of Jewish and American culture, the pioneers served as an agent of acculturation among the newcomers. The early ethnic community provided a reference group for the inhabitants of the larger ghetto of later years. Yet it is the relatively large and homogeneous ethnic colony which has received the major attention of social scientists.

Wieder culled many other significant observations from his lengthy, probing interviews with elderly Jewish men and women who formerly resided in the North End. While there are many possibilities of error in an historical reconstruction of this kind, the author has employed good methodological devices to minimize inaccuracies.

The author brought to his research an intimate familiarity with Eastern European Jewish culture, Yiddish, Orthodox Judaism and the problems of immigrants. His personal history includes an early youth spent in a small Jewish community in Hungary; ordination for the rabbinate; hiding from the Nazis and confinement in concentration camps; and, after World War II, two years of rehabilitative work among Jewish displaced persons After migrating to the United States in 1947, he continued his Hebrew and secular studies at Yeshiva University, earned his M.A. degree at Brandeis University; and is currently teaching at the Hebrew Teachers College and completing his work for a doctorate in Near Eastern and Judaic Studies at Brandeis University.* In addition to these activities, he undertook the study of the North End Jewish community under my supervision when a grant for this research was made to Brandeis University by the Ethel Bresloff Fund, through the cooperation of Colonel Bernard L. Gorfinkle, Executor.

I have enjoyed working with Rabbi Wieder and watching his rapid absorption of sociological theory and method — which were far removed from his previous scholarly training. It was no small feat for a man committed to a sacred, traditional culture to master the austere discipline of social science, with its canons of objectivity, skepticism, cultural relativity and suspension of value-judgment. Yet Wieder did just this in his role of scientist without in any way attenuating the rigor of his orthodoxy in his role of rabbi.

With the author as his guide, I urge the reader to travel back in the reminiscences of elderly men and women to Boston's vanished Jewish community of the North End.

JEROME HIMELHOCH

Goddard College
Plainfield, Vermont
March, 1960

*The doctorate was awarded in June, 1962, subsequent to this writing, on the basis of a dissertation titled JEREMIAH IN AGGA-DIC LITERATURE.

Dr. Himelhoch is Professor of Sociology and Director, Vermont Youth Study, at Goddard College. He was formerly associated with Brandeis University as Assistant Professor of Sociology.

1

scope and methods

THE SUBJECT of this study is the history of the Eastern European Jewish community of the North End in Boston during the last three decades of the nineteenth century. We shall focus upon the social tendencies and religio-cultural attitudes prevailing among the immigrants in that area during the period mentioned.

Our study is based primarily on material gathered by interviews with a number of Boston Jewish citizens of advanced age who were formerly residents of the North End. These people reported both their own recollections and what they remembered having heard from their elders.

There was little in professional literature to guide us in defining the proper technique for such retrospective interviewing.[1] The nature of the subject matter and the age of the respondents made it necessary to make the interviews as informal as possible. At the home of the respondent or at his private business office the interviewee would be encouraged to reminisce aloud for a while about the years he spent in the North End, after which a series of specific questions would be asked.

Interviews lasted from 50 to 130 minutes, with an average length of 80 minutes. A tape recorder was used, but only when permission by the respondent was granted without hesitation. In a few cases when the use of the machine noticeably inhibited the interviewee, the machine was disconnected after ten to fifteen minutes. Twenty people were interviewed in this manner. Shorter less formal interviews were given to an additional large number of old-time Boston Jewish residents.

The selection of interviewees was not based on any detailed pattern established beforehand. North End residence before or around the turn of the century and advanced age were the only requirements we set. Thus, our group of respondents did not constitute a representative sampling of the overall North End Jewish population according to the rigorous standards of present day sociological surveys. For one thing, their advanced age (averaging 79 years) indicated that in respect to physical vigor they were above the ordinary in their generation. Secondly, in this age group our search for would-be interviewees had to be done by recommendation. People would understandably point out to us the more intelligent survivors of those days, especially those who became known in the city by virtue of their profession, their standing in the business world, or their participation in public life. Thus, most of our interviewees were among the more successful former North Enders.

The fact that the object of our scrutiny was a community that existed sixty to ninety years ago created various problems. We were aware of the limitations present in every fact-finding endeavor in which one is to depend on statements made by subjects about their

ancestors and the society of their younger years. Forget-
fulness, involuntary retrospective distortion and the
utterance of evaluative descriptions were some of the
possible pitfalls. On the other hand, a genuine readiness
on the part of the respondents to help the project and
the fact that most of them obviously enjoyed the interview were in our favor.[2] Good rapport was facili-
tated by the acquaintance of the interviewer with
European *shtetl* life as well as with immigrant experience
in general.[3] The interviewer's contact with elderly first
generation Jews, maintained professionally for years, as
well as his ability to use the Yiddish language[4] with
ease further contributed to an atmosphere of mutual understanding. Thus, respondents could speak to the interviewer rather freely without the inhibition (or
attempted embellishment) frequently present when
aged persons try to introduce "the good old times" to
a younger man who is a stranger in their world. It
is hoped that by this analysis of the society of an
early Eastern European Jewish Community in a large
American city, some contribution is being made to
the study of the sociological processes that have been
operating within American Jewry.

2

immigration

THE PARTICULAR SECTION of the Old North End[5] of
Boston in which Jews settled during the last three decades of the nineteenth century was a triangular area, each
side of which measured about one fourth of a mile. The
approximate boundaries of the Jewish neighborhood
were Hanover Street on the southeast, Endicott Street on
the west and Prince Street (in later periods Sheafe and
North Bennet Streets) on the northeast. Salem Street
crossed this area in a southwest-northeast direction.
Smaller thoroughfares, remembered well by former
North Enders, which connected these major streets included Cross Street, Morton Street, Stillman Street,
North Margin Street and Parmenter Street. In addition,
contemporary maps show and interviewees recall a large
number of "places," actually blind alleys, such as Baldwin Place, Salem Place, Noyes Place, Bartlett Place and
many others.

These boundaries could not be set with any rigidity.
We constantly found families who lived in nearby streets
which otherwise had a gentile population. For example,
many Jews established their homes in the area between

the North End and the younger Jewish neighborhood of the West End.[6]

A short distance to the south was the South End neighborhood, whose early Jewish settlers were of German origin. (Many of them did not favor eastern Jews.) North Enders kept up a lively contact with these "coreligionists" as well as those who dwelt in the West End, East Boston and Chelsea.

THE LARGE MAJORITY of the Jews who settled in the North End came from the Russian Empire. White Russia, Ukraine, Lithuania and most of Poland belonged at this time to Russia; Galicia was under the rule of Austria-Hungary. "Since 1869 there had been in progress a slow, but steady, emigration of Russian Jews. . . . This was the beginning of the third wave of Jewish immigration into America, coming on the top of the early Portuguese and the more recent German."[7]

Within Russian Jewry itself, there were divisions based on locality, Yiddish dialect, Hebrew pronunciation and religious traditions. In America, the ones who belonged to the same group tended to form their own synagogues.[8] Although the groups on both the North End and the West End were mixed, some interviewees observed that the North End had more of a *Litvak* character, while the West End had more *Russishe* Jews.

In addition to these groups immigrating from Russia, there were many Hungarians ("We had no use for Hungarians," says one interviewee) and some Oriental Jews. ("They looked awfully dirty in those clothes," remembers another one, "they wore very colorful clothes.") "Outside the main stream of Jewish immigration from Europe were a number of supplementary currents that added to American Jewry nearly fifty thousand 'Oriental' Jews. Natives of Greece and Turkey, Syria and Morocco, their languages Greek, Arabic and Ladino, they joined in the New World other Jews with whom they had little contact for some five hundred years."[9]

It is interesting to note that the area in which East European Jews settled tended to be regarded by outsiders as the Jewish section in town, more than the neighborhood of the German Jews. A contemporary travel guide refers to the North End as "the ghetto," but not to the South End. In a book published in 1883 we read, "There is no distinctively Hebrew quarter although many live on Salem Street and in that immediate neighborhood."[10] The German Jews were by then perhaps sufficiently dispersed in the city not to form a "distinctively Hebrew quarter." A greater degree of adjustment achieved by them may have caused the German Jews to be less noticeable than the newer arrivals.

Various reasons were given by interviewees when asked why their families had left Russia. In earlier years the danger of being drafted in the Russian army — a prospect of unlimited suffering for a Jew — was one of the rather frequent causes for emigration.[11] Beginning with the eighties, the deteriorating conditions of Russian Jewry prompted additional thousands to look westward. "Each new Russian ukase which straitened the living space of the Jews increased the number of those eager to migrate."[12]

Not all, however, left their homes with the purpose of crossing the ocean. Some wanted to settle in Western Europe. Others aspired to reach the land of Israel. The question "Whence comest thou?" was easier to answer than the question "Whither art thou going?" Rabbi

Zalman Yaakov Friederman, one of the scholarly figures of the North End, was dispatched from Kovno by the famed Rabbi Isaac Elchanan to a rabbinic position in Amsterdam. He did not like it there and decided to come to America. The family of Nachman Solomon Rabinowitz left Russia in order to go to Palestine. The father was an ardent *Biluist*[13] who did not give up his hope to reach the Land of the Fathers even after he had landed in America. Another family, that of intellectual Louis Millionthaler, had lived for many years in England before crossing the ocean.

Many immigrants chose Boston as the city of their settlement because their relatives or *landsleit* had lived in this city. Frequently, however, their coming to a given city was purely a matter of coincidence. "Arriving at Castle Garden by the Australia, [Abraham Bilafsky and his family] were 'billeted' to Baltimore, but by a mistake in writing were sent to Boston." As Handlin puts it, "Chance was so large an element in the course of migration, it left little room for planning. The place of landing was less often the outcome of an intention held at the outset of the journey than of blind drift along the routes of trade or of a sudden halt due to the accidents of the voyage."[14]

The "drift along the routes of trade" caused many immigrants to finally settle in Boston, even if they had originally landed elsewhere. Interviewees remember peddlers who came from afar to sell their wares in the Boston area and then simply decided to settle in this city, from which they would be able to reach their customers with greater ease.

What conditions were responsible for the fact that the North End became the neighborhood of Eastern Euro-

The North End is still a neighborhood of first generation Americans — only the nationality has changed.

Ladies on a shopping tour more than six decades ago.

pean Jews? The son of a real estate dealer and builder of the time says: "Perhaps cheaper housing. It was an old colonial neighborhood. By my time, the original families had long moved away. Before the Jews came, it was an Irish neighborhood."

According to another interviewee, "It was close to the waterfront. The South Ferry that connected the city with the Harbor landed at Fleet Street in the North End."

Whatever their reason for choosing this area, in the early seventies a few Jewish families arrived in the North End. An interviewee, who came in 1881, was asked:

Q. When you came to the North End did the area already have a large Jewish population?

A. There must have been forty or fifty families.

Q. Did you hear anything in your childhood as to how much earlier the Jews moved in to the North End?

A. They said that eight to ten years earlier it was all Irish. This was in 1881. So I guess fifty families must have settled there in the 1870's.

The first ones seem to have moved there from the South End. "I started telling you about Henry Wyzansky. He was one of eight or nine brothers. One of his brothers had a butcher store in the South End when Henry came. In 1869 or 1870 he bought (or perhaps hired first) a house on 5 Stillman Street and opened downstairs a butcher store of his own. Many of the newcomers came to his house when they arrived. Many immigrants lived with him for a considerable period of time. They paid him three dollars a week for room and board. Most of them were not relatives."

For almost three decades these early settlers and a comparatively small number of others who followed them lived scattered among the Irish inhabitants of the

North End. The crowded, all-Jewish North End, so well known to Boston Jews around and after the turn of the century, had not yet emerged. In 1873 a congregation was founded by one of the early arrivals in the area.[15] The founder's daughter remembers however that even after a few years of the existence of this congregation she was sometimes sent to neighbors' homes to call someone to the *minyan*. A North End girl who was married in 1887 had difficulty finding an apartment on Salem Street "because she was Jewish." Another former resident, who came as late as 1897, writes: "As I recall the North End of those days, it was still a good residential section of the city. Although the neighborhood was predominantly Irish, with a scattering of Jewish families, there were also a number of old homes occupied by descendants of the original owners, who themselves were pretty well along in years. . . . The change in the neighborhood was marked even before my graduation from the Hancock School in 1904 and by the time I had graduated from high school, the Irish had all but disappeared from the North End and were rapidly being replaced by a large Jewish population."[16]

The change in the picture of the North End between the 1870's and the 1900's can best be illustrated by comparing two statements made by interviewees. One relates that his mother, who went to school after 1870, could find only Irish playmates at school. The other, a physician, tells me that in the early 1900's he was once sent out from his medical school to supervise a birth at a North End home. On the way he saw a trio of boys consisting of a Jewish, an Irish and a Negro boy. They were arguing in a loud voice — in Yiddish.

Thus, the character of the North End Jewish community during the first period of its history was very different from what it was to become after the turn of the century. The earlier community was small in numbers, struggling to maintain its institutions. It was not yet a "Jewish neighborhood"; they were still a minority. It leaned in many ways on the older German community in other parts of the city. Its members were "a friendly lot," "a very homogeneous group." They "were as happy as they could be in those days." Their initial poverty was soon overcome. They Americanized fast. Unlike the later immigrants, they remained in the North End for a long time. When the large influx began, these early inhabitants became in many ways the guides of the new arrivals. In view of this role and in view of the fact that they were the first to confront the enormous problems of the Jewish immigrant in an area hitherto devoid of Jews, they perhaps deserve the appellation "pioneers" (using this word in a considerably extended sense) which their descendants today affectionately apply to them. The presence of such a smaller, better Americanized community, settled in an area before the beginning of large scale immigration, may have important implications for the sociological processes in the later immigrant group, such as the speed and the mode of its acculturation. We shall touch on these implications in a later section after we have described North End Jewish life in detail according to its major institutional areas.

3

making a living

WHAT WERE THE OCCUPATIONS of the North End Jews at the end of the nineteenth century?[17] As in the case of many other aspects of immigrant life, the economic activities of the first generation Jews were determined by two sets of factors: on the one hand by the background the immigrants brought with them from the old world, and on the other hand by the particular conditions under which they were to begin their money-earning career in the new land. The Jewish immigrants started on their westward journey from the same place as that in which other immigrant groups had their origin: from the European village or small town.[18] The role of the Jew in the economic life of the village had, however, differed from the role of the peasant. This had an effect on the choice of occupations by the Jews in the new world. They did not become farming colonists because even in Europe most of them did not engage in agriculture. The few attempts to settle Jews on the soil in the new world met with limited success.[19] Despite an avidity for learning inspired by their faith, the educated professions remained closed to them until their descendants, reared in the culture of the new land, would attain a place in those fields. The economic area to which the Jews were accustomed from home and which fit the needs of the Jewish immigrants was, in the main, small trade. At the time of their arrival, small trade was practiced in America by Jewish immigrants in the form of peddling,[20] although many became small storekeepers. One interview contains the following discussion:

Q. What occupations did the North End Jews have outside of peddling?

A. Well, they had stores; my father never peddled.

Q. I know. But would you say that a large percentage of the people had stores or a small percentage?

A. No, I would say a small percentage. A large percentage were peddlers. Everybody who came to America, who came to Boston, would take a basket.

Q. Would you say that 80% of the people peddled or more or less?

A. Well, it would be only a guess on my part. All I can remember is . . . about a handful of store-keepers and everybody else . . . coming and filling the baskets.

Without the knowledge of the language, without any capital, a young immigrant would still be able to "fill up a basket" of merchandise on credit, set out on the road and sell his wares.[21] In the beginning he was not able even to name in English the needles, ribbons, shoelaces and yarns he had to offer. One interviewee recalls that one of the first sentences of English a new arrival would be taught in the North End was "Look in the basket." Jewish peddler and Yankee or Irish customer were socially and culturally worlds apart, yet commercial talent, good merchandise and a desire to please created a bridge of successful trading between the former *kremer* of the Russian village and the New England farmer or factory worker who was to become in a short time a trusting customer.

The basket-peddler carried small inexpensive articles. More valuable merchandise would be sold by the peddler who carried a "pack on the back." The pack would contain pillow cases, sheets, aprons, towels, dresses and other similar articles. One interviewee remembers that his father would walk with pack on his back from the North End to Hyde Park. His burden would be increased by the kosher food he had to take along from home. He would not buy even bread on the road. The wares were acquired from one of the few peddlers' supply stores in the North End. A son of the owner of one of the largest among these establishments describes the credit arrangements of the typical newcomer in the following excerpt:

Q. You said that many North Enders peddled after landing in America. Was there no need for a certain amount of capital even for that small business activity?

A. I can tell you how it worked in my father's store. I told you that he had a peddlers' supply store. When an immigrant arrived and wanted merchandise for peddling, they would talk to him and if he appeared honest they would give him fifty dollars credit. When he paid the amount, he would get more credit.

Q. How would he know where to peddle?

A. Other peddlers would tell him of some "uncharted" neighborhood which was not visited yet by many peddlers and where prospects were good. It was not easy to acquire customers. But once they knew you, you could make money.

Q. Was that because of a considerable margin of profit?

A. It was mainly because the peddler sold on an installment plan. The Irish woman would buy an item and the peddler would collect every week a small amount for it. Over a considerable stretch of time he collected a profit above the original fifty dollars which he received in merchandise for credit.

In addition to the basket peddler and the "pack-on-back" peddler there was the "tin-peddler" who sold kitchen utensils. Moreover, even groceries were sometimes sold by North End peddlers. The great advancement in the lot of a peddler was when he was able to acquire a "horse and buggy" and carry with greater ease a much larger assortment of wares.

An experienced peddler sometimes employed other newcomers — beginners in the trade — to sell his wares. This could grow into big business. One resident speaks of a relative who had twenty peddlers distributing his merchandise. The wave of immigration toward the end of the century resulted in the establishment of many boarding and lodging houses. The landladies of these houses were in constant need of linens, soaps and even groceries. To enlist some of these landladies as one's customers would be particularly lucrative. Later, the "customer-peddler" came. His clients were mainly city dwellers or farmers from nearby locations. He carried only samples. When the Irish woman chose a dress from among these samples, she was given a written order to a store in town. She received her dress there, for which the peddler was billed at a wholesale price. She then paid for the dress in installments to the peddler, who thus made his profit.

Peddling was, of course, a strenuous occupation. Residents recall the long line of peddlers gathered on Saturday nights at peddlers' supply stores to have their baskets filled. The journey would start early on Sunday mornings and sometimes last an entire week. On Fridays they would return exhausted, hungry for a warm meal but with a few dollars of profit. The latter would be divided into three parts. Some of it would be used for living expenses; some would be re-invested in new merchandise; a third part would almost invariably be deposited with the steamship ticket agent toward the expense of bringing over some loved one from the other side.[22] There is no wonder that they were eager to exchange this type of life for a more settled one. When the peddler accumulated sufficient funds, he opened a small store on Salem Street, usually in a basement made fit by one of the landlords. Frequently, the store had two counters, in which case it was shared by two "businessmen" for the sale of non-competing products. Their customers were by no means only Jewish. In their peddling days they learned well the art of small trading with the Irish and the Italians. They continued to use that ability to advantage in the new store.

At other times, a number of peddlers pooled their funds to establish a peddlers' supply store. From their own experience they knew what their peddler friends needed. The increase in immigration — which meant an increase in the number of peddlers — thus resulted in excellent opportunities for the former immigrants to become wholesalers of all kinds. In addition to the rather large firm of the Freedman Brothers, interviewees mention the store of Louis Berenson, the one owned by Harris Gorfinkle and Company (established in 1888 by eight former peddlers) which distributed women's clothing, that of Richmond, Cohen, and Reinherz, which specialized in men's clothing, as well as the store owned by Michael Slutsky.

The owners of the peddlers' supply stores constituted a financially and socially leading group among the North End Jews. Next to them on the social ladder were the owners of the retail stores. As one North Ender puts it: ". . . Of course, there were strata within the Jewish population: men who had the stores, men who worked manually and the poor people who were unable to do anything."

Q. Where did the peddlers belong?

A. One step below the storekeepers.

Q. What kind of manual work did the second group do?

A. They were tailors, shoemakers and some who began to get work outside the locale.

Trade was thus by no means the only occupation North End Jews were engaged in. Immigrants sometimes tried their luck in many different fields of endeavor until they found a fitting occupation for themselves. The recollection of the son of one of them is characteristic: "Father worked in an iron foundry at Charlestown. Later, he became a street-car conductor. Finally, he had a horse-drawn taxicab, a "herdicle." After these jobs he became a *shames* at a Lithuanian synagogue."

In contrast to this immigrant, I. B. Reinherz, one of the leading figures in that community, started in the new world with an occupation related to religious life, that of *shoichet*, and only later did he transfer to the secular calling of steamship ticket agent and banker. Other immigrants remembered by interviewees were engaged in the real estate business, which promised good opportunities for earning in view of the expected large-scale immigration. "I went into architecture because my father not only bought real estate but also built and remodeled. I was interested in art and that sort of thing."

Soon after their arrival, some early immigrants opened small tailor shops, some of which later grew into large establishments with the emergence of the Jewish needle industry.

The Eastern European *balagole* had his American counterpart in the Jewish driver of the horse-drawn cabs of the time. There was a stand of these cabs on Postoffice Square and many North End Jews could be found among the drivers.

Business morality—as viewed, perhaps a bit benevolently, by former residents — was generally on a high level. "The Jews in those days who used to live down there were very honorable. In those days my father couldn't believe in a second mortgage. That was swindling, he thought." Yet even this society had its share of those who liked to earn easy money. One interviewee relates: "There were, however, other occupations. There were some money lenders, not too well liked or respected. There was a certain [name omitted], known as the 'old clothes man' among Harvard students. He would buy the used clothes of wealthy students who had come to the end of their money allowances. It was easier for these students to convince their parents to buy them a new suit than to get them to send extra pocket money.

He would also make loans to students to be paid after the next visit home or even after graduation."

In conclusion: The manner in which the first generation immigrant earned his living was determined by the conditions and opportunities of America's contemporary economy and by the abilities, experiences and goals which the immigrants brought over with them. They embarked on careers in which the use of their "imported" resources promised greatest success in view of American economic reality. Small trade in the earlier periods, certain forms of industrial employment in the later years seemed to be the forms of earning that suited them best.

Peddling — the prevalent form of small trade — had a double advantage. On the one hand it was in many ways a continuation of small-town trading Jews had practiced in Europe. On the other hand it helped in the limited and gradual acculturation the immigrants desired. As pointed out in another section of this study, there are many indications that the attitude of immigrants to acculturation was much more favorable than is commonly recognized. They adhered to forms brought over with them from the old country but they prepared themselves for changes in their way of life, or in the way of life of their children, which appeared to them inevitable in the new world. Peddling, which helped them get acquainted with America better than anything else, became in their lives not only an important economic but also a welcome Americanizing factor. It provided an opportunity to keep daily contact with non-Jewish Americans, to learn their language and their ways. Yet, this contact would be limited to the field of business and would not interfere with the separateness which the immigrant desired to maintain at this time in the religious and social spheres. He observed the vast new world of America, he spoke to the farmer, his wife and his daughter, yet he was only a visitor, a trader perhaps welcome and liked, but always distant.

The ambition and aggressiveness with which the immigrants seem to have set out on their new careers indicates the profound trust they had in their own future in the new land. They spent weeks on the road or stood all hours behind the counter because they knew that their toil would bring financial rewards they could never attain in the old country. It must not be forgotten that the prospect of such financial success had been one of the most tempting aspects of America and had provided many an immigrant with the motive to migrate. One may contrast the apathy, the lack of productivity in the economic life of the *shtetl* with the busy liveliness displayed by the former Jews of the *shtetl* once they confronted the challenge and the promise of the demanding, yet free, economy of America. The economic aggressiveness of first generation North End Jews was later transmitted to the second. This process probably contributed to the great advances in the commercial and industrial life of the city of Boston made by the children of many North Enders.

The preoccupation of the immigrant with establishing a livelihood had, however, negative results as well. It was responsible for a rising materialism in a Jewish society in which religion, education and other idealistic pursuits formerly had a much more significant role. The *talmid chochom*, the learned man, was still greatly respected; yet the *amhoretz*, the unlearned Jew, who had been treated with light contempt in the *shtetl*, could much more frequently become an important man in the community if he proved to be a successful peddler.[23]

The strenuous working patterns of the times brought about certain changes in family and community life as well as in leisure-time practices. Fathers saw their children only on the Sabbath. Matters pertaining to the education of the young, to charity and to synagogue activities passed little by little from the hands of the busy menfolk to the hands of the women. One North End rabbi writes in 1908: "Since men are generally engrossed in their business and in their craft, women have a major part in all institutions and charitable activities. [Men] seek rest and repose and habitually say [to one who attempts to involve them in community projects] 'Here is a dollar and leave me alone'."[24]

These other aspects of North End Jewish life will be discussed in the following chapters.

◻◻◻◻◻◻◻◻◻◻◻◻◻◻◻◻◻◻◻◻◻

4

homes and family life

THE HOUSES which the North End Jewish immigrants occupied were in the beginning rather small, insufficiently equipped dwellings.[25] They were not very well suited to give comfort to the immigrant's family, his boarders and his relatives who followed him to America and stayed with him until they had their own homes. Most houses in the area had been built by the earlier Yankee inhabitants who were later displaced by the Irish and the Italians. They were dilapidated but sturdy in basic structure, so that Jewish home owners and real estate dealers found it possible to rebuild them more than once to provide more apartments per house and to make them more livable.[26]

One of the aged interviewees recalls: "Life was very primitive. Toilet was out in the yard. There was running water in the homes but no bath tubs. We would go to [the] American House [on Hanover Street] and take a hot bath [for a small fee]."

In another interview:

Q. How were housing conditions in the North End?

A. Very modest. We lived on an upper floor apartment. People lived even in the attic.

Some real estate men began building "apartment houses," which were distinguished from "tenement houses" mainly by the comforts found in them. According to one interviewee — the son of a North End real estate man — the first apartment house in the area was built in 1885 on the corner of Hanover and Cross Streets.

In these homes the immigrant women went about solving the initial problems of housekeeping with the same determination with which their husbands approached the hardships of earning a livelihood. The desire to make their household Jewish did not make their task easier. For kosher meat they had to walk long distances. At a rather early date, however, a kosher butcher store was established by one of the Wyzanski brothers. Many other products could be purchased on the market place just as in Europe. This is what a lady interviewee has to say about the very early years: "Someone sold chickens on Salem Street, in the backyards. The women would go there and look at them and feel them and they would pick one and the woman would bring the chicken to the [shoichet's] house [to be ritually slaughtered]."

Q. Did they buy chicken only for the Sabbath or for week-days as well?

A. Mainly for *shabes*. Everyone would have chicken and *tsholent* for *shabes*.

Q. Was food expensive?

A. Chicken cost ten to twelve cents a pound. I remember how everyone complained about an inflation when a dozen of eggs went up to twenty cents.

Kosher restaurants served as important
meeting places for early immigrants.
Note both English and Yiddish window inscriptions.

Peddling was an important economic activity in the North End.

Q. How about other food?

A. Fruits were sold in front of the stores. They would sometimes sell you half an orange, if you did not want to buy a whole one.

Most interviewees give the impression that food was adequately available. However, some items which are today within reach even for the poorest were then regarded as luxuries.

Q. What standard of living resulted from these peddling activities? Was there, for example, meat available every day?

A. I do not remember; I know there was chicken for the Sabbath.

Q. Did children buy ice cream as easily as they do nowadays?

A. Ice cream was a rarity. I do not think I had it more frequently than once a month. You offered it to visitors as a refreshment.

These standards of living, regarded as humble by former residents looking back on the past, must have represented to the immigrants themselves a degree of plenty rarely experienced before. *Dos Goldene Land* demanded hard work but promised an opportunity to overcome poverty — the greatest of the social ailments of the *shtetl*.

While the material conditions of home life were to most immigrants better than in Eastern Europe, it was not easy for them to re-create in the new land the characteristic atmosphere of the Jewish home which was present in the tiny dwellings of the old country. Family life was exposed to many trials and changes in the first years after immigration.[27]

For one thing, a large percentage of the immigrants spent years in America without their families. Men alone came "to look around" or to gather the funds necessary for the purchase of steamship tickets for the rest of the family. Some immigrants originally viewed their coming here only as a money-earning venture at the completion of which they planned to return and not bring over their families at all. After these long interruptions, readjustment to affectionate, orderly family life was not always easy. The boarding house was a poor substitute for home and did not make better fathers of the lonely men. Even those who came with wife and children were frequently away on week-long peddling trips. Store-keepers spent their evenings at business and saw their children only on the Sabbath.

The charitable organizations were burdened by the care of many families deserted by the husband and father. "Although Jews had shown a lower rate of desertion than some immigrant groups, it was one of the major problems confronting the Benevolent Association."[28] The occurrence of these cases among Jews was a symptom of the general crisis to which Jewish family life was exposed at this time.

Religious life must have exercised a steadying influence under these conditions. The Sabbath and the holidays, which forced a much needed rest upon everyone, brought the members of the families together for holiday meals and for prayer.[29] Former residents still recall the festivity and the warmth of the home atmosphere which they experienced on these occasions. One elderly lady still sings the Sabbath table songs that she heard at her father's house every Friday evening. Another interviewee recalls his father's Yom Kippur Eve blessing.

When the candles were lit and everyone was ready for *shul*, his father came in dressed in white (apparently in a *kitl*, a special white gown for High Holidays worn by laymen and rabbis alike) and blessed each child separately. (Experiences of this kind may have helped shape the nostalgic type of religiosity which later characterized the otherwise radically unobservant second generation.)

The relationship between the members of the family at first differed little from what it used to be in East European society. Parental authority was high; the American born generation was not yet grown to label its elders old fashioned and foreign. As one interviewee describes her, the mother was usually "the old fashioned type. She was an indefatigable worker. But she accepted at all times the decisions of the father." Frequently, however, interviewees speak of North End women who earned a living for their families, especially by occupations in which Jewish women had been often engaged in Europe as well. Energetic Yente Rabinowitz opened a small grocery store soon after her family arrived in this country. Bernard Berenson, the noted art critic, used to bring his friends to the luncheonette run by his mother.

In most cases, however, the role of the woman was confined to the task of creating a warm home environment for her husband and children who were daily exposed to the bewildering strangeness of the new world. The relationships within the typical North End Jewish home are well characterized in this excerpt: "They had a home life far different than they have now."

Q. In what way?

A. Well, the man, when he came home — that was dinnertime for all. If he came at eight o'clock at night that was all right too. Children had a lot of respect for their parents. What their father said was just so. Mothers, in most cases, were easy-going, always protecting their children in every way.

Q. [In those days] was there any greater significance in the role of the mother?

A. Oh, definitely. As I see it today. Well, I think that the love for the family was greater in those days than today. But the general habits of the women of those days were different . . . they were not going out. I don't remember my mother going out. Never; always at home.

The process of Americanization was bound to force a change upon the position of father, mother, and American born (or at least American-educated) children within the Jewish family. Husbands Americanized faster than their wives. Immigrant men had more contact with the "outside" world than women. On their peddling trips, they were more likely to be influenced by the ways and ideas of the great new world in which they labored for a living. Thus, until the children grew up, the father was the most "modern" member of the family, the recognized expert on all things progressive, American and worldly. The mother, on the other hand, tended to become the guardian of the more familial, more permanent values. She was anxious to secure the continuity of the traditional family atmosphere — thus, she became the conservative force in the family. As a result, we find the mother in the North End in charge of the Jewish education of her children and of many religious and charitable activities in the community. This was in complete contrast with the usual situation back home in the *shtetl*, where all matters pertaining to religious and educational life were the domain of men. The fact that the extreme burden of earning a living left the men little time to occupy themselves with spiritual and cultural matters is only part of the explanation. The resulting general progressive worldliness of men against the traditionalism of women is, I believe, an aspect of the situation to be recognized.[30]

The great events of family life — weddings, Bar Mitzvahs, funerals — were observed among the North End Jews in a manner that greatly differed from the patterns familiar to their descendants today. During the decades that followed the immigration of the East European Jewish masses, many practices were taken over from the gentile environment which for centuries were regarded as "un-Jewish." Making arrangements for the observance of sad or joyous events became, by practical necessity, the task of such businessmen as funeral directors and caterers. In the social atmosphere of the new world, where following "American" and "progressive" ways was a matter of prestige, it became good business to introduce new forms into the consecrated ancient rituals and to sell them as the "new style" and the "modern way." Rabbis of all shades helped this process along sometimes willingly, sometimes reluctantly. As a result, the Jewish wedding ceremony and funeral service and even certain aspects of the Bar Mitzvah celebration in America became, in the course of time, a rather curious mixture of Jewish tradition with numerous other elements coming from varied cultural sources. In the North End, however, this change had not yet taken place.

The elaborate marching preceding the wedding ceremony was not practiced at all. Two *unterfirers* (escorts) led the bride and the groom to the traditional *chupe* (wedding canopy). Two couples were usually honored as *unterfirers*. The two men escorted the groom, the two women led the bride. The two couples were most frequently the parents of groom and bride. There was music and much dancing at weddings. "They frequently performed *kazatzkis*." One interviewee speaks of much dancing of men and women together: somewhat surprising for the times. He adds, however, that *his* parents never danced together. Weddings were usually held at the synagogue, both the religious ceremony and the reception. "The Baldwin Place synagogue had a dining hall. Later the more free-circulating people would go to some of the halls on the South End."

Boys were circumcized at home and given a Hebrew name by a *moihel* (ritual circumcisor) in the area. Girls were named in the synagogue usually on a Sabbath morning. Parties would follow both events.

Bar Mitzvah celebrations were simpler and more dignified than the extravagant affairs in vogue today. A "speech" was delivered by the boy in Yiddish, sometimes in English, rarely in Hebrew. The rabbi did not address the Bar Mitzvah boy. Bar Mitzvah parties took the form of Sabbath dinners following services.

In the beginning, no Jewish funeral homes existed in the area. Funeral processions would depart from the home of the deceased. As in Europe, the members of the Chevrah Kadisha (Holy Society: a society of laymen dedicated to the reverent care of the dead and to the practice of other deeds of kindness) performed all duties in preparation for the funeral. They bathed and clothed the body of the deceased, prepared the traditional white shrouds and sometimes even made the simple coffin.

They were guided in all this by the sextons of the synagogues who gradually took over more and more of these duties from the busy lay members of the Chevrah. Later some of these sextons established their own funeral parlors. The founders of two Jewish funeral homes at present operating in Boston were the sextons of two neighboring North End synagogues.

5

religious life

THE RELIGIOUS ATTITUDES and practices of first generation Eastern European immigrants, settled in their own
neighborhood in an American city, are of great significance in a study of immigrant adjustment. The culture
that these newcomers brought with them had been es-
sentially a religious culture. The shaping of their
religious life in the new land constitutes an important
aspect of their adjustment.[31]

What former North Enders have to say about religious
life in that area seems to indicate that the last quarter of
the nineteenth century was, for the members of the first
generation, a period of two contradictory tendencies.[32]
Externally, they attempted to retain the patterns of
European Jewish life; while, in their thinking, they
made themselves ready for a drastic acculturation that
would become visible only in the second generation.

The evolution in their ideology had begun even while
they were making concerted efforts to retain in an un-
changed form all institutions and practices that made up
their religious life in the old home. The members of this
community, with few exceptions, conformed in their ex-

ternal conduct to the code of religious behavior transplanted from the Russian small town. Yet, the ferment of a desire for, or at least an acceptance of change was at work in the minds of the people of the first generation themselves. Its consequences would become observable in the almost complete break with religious discipline made by their children.

The son of one of the pious and learned leaders of the Chevra Shas (Talmudical Society) reports, for example: "While Father observed all religious rites in every possible way . . . nevertheless . . . he would make certain statements . . . that indicated to me that his ideas were entirely liberal. But living in a community as he was he naturally followed the dictates . . . of the community."[33] While most interviewees depict the youth of the North End as observant only to a very limited degree, they do not seem to remember any significant tension between these young people and their pious parents. On the contrary: "The older generation gradually accepted the ways of their children. They knew they could not remain as orthodox [sic]. They were not too willing, but they knew it had to come." This creeping religious liberalism of many in the first generation — frequently thought, occasionally spoken, but rarely practiced — did not always originate on American soil. The ideas the eighteenth and nineteenth century had brought to Europe did not remain outside the limits of the *shtetl*. Many immigrants brought with them a familiarity with these ideas. The American milieu, with its emphasis on freedom, gave such "enlightened" ideas a better chance than they ever had in the deeply traditional, learned, pious and considerably rigid environment of the small town. The presence of a strong Reform movement in the midst of the older German-Jewish community helped this process immensely. Laxity in ritual practice — despised by the society of the Russian small town — had in the new world the prestige of being acceptable to a large part of the older, wealthier, already Americanized community.

As we said before, the results of this process became evident only when the second generation came into its own. The North End Jews of the last decades of the century were, by and large, a traditional group in which observance was to remain the norm for a long time.

Although their orthodoxy had more to do with a traditionalism of habit than with any systematic ideology of observance, still their rejection of Reform was unequivocal. This rejection, however, was rarely given literary expression, at least not in English. An exception was a little pamphlet, written in an erudite English by a former North End Jew, Louis Millionthaler, grandfather of Bernard L. Gorfinkle, in 1901. The author, who was "looked upon with much regard among his people as a good Hebrew and as a scholar," refuted a suggestion by Rabbi Charles Fleischer of Congregation Adath Israel that henceforth the founder of Christianity should be regarded "as a Jew of the Jews and should rank with Moses and with Jacob as a prophet and as a doer of good." This booklet was considered "a bombshell shot from the camp of the Orthodox into that of the Reform Hebrews,"[34] although Rabbi Fleischer's idea did not reflect the stand of the entire Reform spiritual leadership.

Besides the traditionally minded majority there was, even during that period, a small minority who held militant anti-religious views.[35] One interviewee remembers that his grandfather never went to Shul even during

47

the High Holidays. He had come from a family of "atheists" — "they liked Voltaire and Renan." There were many *Maskilim* (followers of the *Haskalah*, a Jewish movement of "enlightenment"). Socialism, rapidly spreading among American Jews during the years of massive immigration, became a powerful vehicle for irreligiosity. One North Ender recalls "a small group of a violently anti-religious philosophy. They would defiantly arrange a ball on Yom Kippur eve while most Jews attended the Kol Nidre services. During Yom Kippur day they would stand on the street and eat ham sandwiches."

These minorities — vociferous though they were — did not, however, perceptibly change the general picture of the North End as a community observing religious law. According to the majority of interviewees, "everybody" observed the Sabbath and "all" homes were Kosher. One former resident recalls, however, that "these contractors worked on the Sabbath." ("These contractors" are defined by him as "tailors who would contract for making . . . suits for [various business establishments] in town.") The son of a builder and real estate dealer remembers that his father kept his store open while other stores were closed . . . "My father was a very, very liberal man. [He] was [in liberal ideas] way ahead of everybody." It seems that the owners of retail stores — dependent as they were more than any other occupational group on the patronage of the community — held out longest in their observance of the Seventh Day. One interviewee remembers the first occasion when a store dared to open in the North End on a Sabbath. This happened in 1903. "There was a riot. Windows were smashed and police had to be called." A

similar public reaction is reported by another interviewee to have been felt when a delicatessen store once
opened on Yom Kippur earlier than nightfall.

Banks did not differ from small stores in this respect.[36]
I. B. Reinherz's prosperous combination of bank and
ticket agency was closed every Sabbath. North Enders
recall that policemen were regularly stationed near the
establishment on Saturday nights to keep order among
the crowd assembled there. Clients were anxious to take
care of their business as soon as the doors opened after
the appearance in the sky of the three stars which, by
Jewish law, mark the end of the Sabbath. The Cunard
steamship lines once made an offer to Reinherz to make
his bank the exclusive agency for the lines. One of the
lines' conditions was that his business be kept open on
the Sabbath. He would not consider such a condition
and the offer was rejected.

The first Jewish services in the North End were probably held in private homes where friends gathered on the
mornings of holidays to worship under the leadership of
more learned settlers. A Torah-scroll would be borrowed
from one of the older South End synagogues and a worshiper would be found who could read it. We may assume that during ordinary weekday or Sabbath services
almost any worshiper could act as a *chazn*. Reading the
vowel-less text of the Torah with the proper chant was
more difficult. I. B. Reinherz was a good *baal kerieh*
(Torah-reader). He later acted as such in the Baldwin
Place synagogue. As early as 1873 Congregation Beth
Abraham was founded by the Reinherz family.[37] Until
1890 — when Congregation Beth Israel opened its synagogue on Baldwin Place — Beth Abraham was the leading place of worship.

In addition to these larger, central synagogues, the increase of immigration caused various groups to form small temporary congregations. They usually hired a "hall" for the High Holidays when prospective worshipers were numerous, then continued to assemble the congregation during the rest of the year in a home, a basement, or a rented store.[38] *Landsmannschaften* or various other societies sponsored these religious activities. The Agudah Leumit — a cultural, Zionist group of younger immigrants — sponsored such a *minyan* on Hanover Street. After the fast on Yom Kippur, when the services were over, the Ark was removed and a joyous celebration followed.

How well were the synagogues attended? One interviewee recalls that she was frequently sent out as a little girl to call a neighbor over for the *minyan*. This was before the great wave of immigration began. Around the turn of the century — another former resident tells me — there were several successive services held at the Baldwin Place synagogue even on an ordinary weekday morning. "On Saturday, when leaving the synagogue, it appeared like a real parade. Silk hats, holiday garments, and many long *kapotes*."

To the early settlers the synagogue meant much more than just a place of worship. Before and after the services, worshipers discussed all matters that were vital to them in the new world. The stranger, whom a long business trip brought to Boston, stopped first at the synagogue to inquire about lodging in a Jewish home. Here they exchanged experiences gained in peddling, gave advice and encouragement to the newcomers, received news about home and about *landsleit* who dwelt in other cities.

The synagogue was for a long time the only place where the immigrants' cultural needs could be satisfied. Many lectures and adult classes were held on its premises. For the learned, this was the place where their knowledge would be recognized and appreciated. Since Hebrew books were scarce, the synagogue's *sforim* (Hebrew volumes) purchased with great sacrifice, rendered an invaluable service to former students of European *yeshivas* and *chadorim*. An unskilled laborer or a struggling peddler would earn the esteem of his fellow Jews if he was able to answer a knotty question of law or explain a difficult passage of the Talmud.

Within the synagogues, small auxiliary groups were formed to satisfy specific religious or educational needs. Members of the Chevra Tehillim assembled at given times to recite certain portions of the Hebrew Book of Psalms. When one of their rank died, other members were on hand to read Psalms in unison at the home of the deceased or at the funeral chapel. The North End congregation known as Chevra Tehillim originally evolved from such a Psalm reading society.

The Chevra Shas, a society for the study of the Talmud, counted among its members the most learned of the Jewish population. I. B. Reinherz founded the first Chevra Shas shortly after 1873.[39] (According to the writer of the article on Boston in the encyclopedia *Ozar Yisrael* — himself a North End rabbi of the time — this Chevra Shas brought to Boston a set of the Talmud for the first time in the city's history. This statement, if correct, would lead us to the somewhat surprising conclusion that the earlier German Jewish communities never owned a set of the Talmud.)

Synagogue services followed the Eastern European

pattern. All prayers were said in Hebrew. Prayerbooks had no translation or Yiddish translations only. Prayerbooks with German or English translations that happened to find their way to North End synagogues were looked upon by newcomers with curiosity as strange products of the new world. Indeed, their pages, on which the sacred words appeared side by side with the unknown non-Jewish print, became, in their eyes, symbols of the diluted new-world Jewishness they had been warned against before leaving the old home.

Bearded, skull-capped merchant and
youthful customer in the old North End.

Corner of Salem and Prince Streets, North End, one of the oldest apothecary stores in Boston.

□□□□□□□□□□□□□□□□□□□□□□□□□□□

6

raising a new generation

IN CHOOSING THE FORM of a Jewish education for their
children, the immigrants attempted to copy the patterns familiar to them from the old world, as they did
in other matters pertaining to Jewish life. Most of them
were used to having their offspring taught by a privately
paid *rebbe* (teacher) who set up school in one of the
rooms of his not-too-comfortable home. Periodically
the child would bring along installments of the tuition
fee (*rebbe-gelt* or *sechar-limud*) set aside from the parents'
earnings, often with great sacrifice. Schools of this type
(called *chadorim*, plural of *cheder*) were the first institutions of Hebrew education to appear in the North End.[40]
One of the first *chadorim* was conducted by Abraham
Reinherz.

The number of these schools multiplied with the increased immigration after the eighties. At that time various *chadorim* seem to have been in existence. While
there were no grades, each *cheder* was concentrating on
one phase of instruction only. Some taught the youngest
children to read the *Siddur*, others taught older ones to
translate the Bible. One interviewee even remembers

gemore-melamdim, teachers who taught the Talmud. Thus, the advancement of a student was indicated by the fact that he was able to change from a *cheder* where *Ivre* (Hebrew Reading) was taught to one in which *Chumesh* (the Books of the Pentateuch) constituted the curriculum. Translation was usually from Hebrew to Yiddish. However, in some "modern" *chadorim* the Bible was translated, even at that period, into English. In some *chadorim* teaching was intensive. Hebrew education began at an earlier age than English. Even while they went to public school, many children spent "a few hours" every afternoon at the *cheder*. One interviewee recalls, "I knew how to read and translate the Five Books [of Moses] when I was eight years old." His statement is not necessarily exaggerated. Neither is this something that could happen "only in those days." Similar results can be observed today in any one of the European-type schools maintained by *Chassidim* in many Brooklyn neighborhoods, for example. A good description of North End *chadorim* is given by this excerpt from an interview:

Q. You were, at that time, just about eight years old. Did you go to Hebrew school?

A. Yes. I went to Lubitsky's *cheder*. The old Lubitsky had an ordinary old-fashioned *cheder*. But his son ran a "modern" type of *cheder*. He had a real classroom with seats and a blackboard.

Q. How were the ordinary *chadorim* equipped?

A. There was no school furniture in them. The rabbi had a big table and the children sat around. Sometimes the table reached up to the chin of the smaller children. The rabbi read the Bible and translated it into Jewish. There was no blackboard.

54

Q. Who ran these *chadorim?*

A. I told you about the two Lubitsky's. Another one was run by a man named Zussman.

Q. What was the age of children going to these private Hebrew schools?

A. Seven to thirteen or fourteen.

Q. Did anyone continue Jewish education after that age?

A. I remember no one.

Q. You said these schools were "private." Do you mean that the parents paid tuition to the rabbi directly?

A. Yes, they would pay twenty-five to fifty cents a week. But in young Lubitsky's *cheder* the price was high: fifty cents. He even took the children on outings in the summer to Middlesex Falls.

Q. Were there any community sponsored Jewish educational institutions?

A. Let me tell you something interesting in this connection. There was a very excellent retired Christian businessman in the North End, a Mr. Samuel F. Hubbard. He was the superintendent of the North End Union. He had a great influence on the children. He taught them integrity and the value of being educated. He asked me in 1903 why it was that Reform temples neglected the Jewish education of children. This remark was brought by me to the attention of a Zionist conference and the result was that a resolution was adopted urging Zionists all over the country to become active in the field of Jewish education. Later the members of the Sons of Zion asked the Baldwin Place Synagogue to establish a school in the synagogue building. But it was only a Sunday School.

From time to time similar attempts were made to open

community sponsored Hebrew schools. "In Cockrow Hall, corner of Richmond and Hanover Street, there was a *shul* one year. They had a Hebrew school. Sam Kronberg was a teacher." The Tulmud Torah at 287 ½ Hanover Street opened in 1883 under the presidency of H. M. Hillson. "With eighty pupils in 1885 it struggled to maintain itself until 1893, helped from time to time by generous subscriptions of prospering North Enders. The trials of this school were typical of many small educational projects of the refugees in each successive year."[40a] The Baldwin Place Synagogue also maintained a *cheder* at one time. The *shames* acted as the teacher.

The "staff" of all these schools did not consist of trained educators. In Europe, the parents in the *shtetl* could at least choose from among the many villagers who offered their talents as *melamdim*. Even though no one had any "diploma," the parents selected the ones who, by their piety, their knowledge, their "feel" for the children, seemed most suitable. In America, these qualities were not abundantly available in the prospective educators. One interviewee says: "Teachers would usually be older men. Immigrants would sometimes start earning their livelihood by teaching.[41] A few teachers were able to speak to children in English. Frequent punishment was part of all Hebrew school life."[42]

The more learned parents followed the progress of their children with attention. The father saw his children mainly on the Sabbath. It was his practice to examine the youngster on that day. "Every Friday evening [my father] would take me upstairs in my house and I had to go through the *Sidrah* of the following morning."

There were other typically European arrangements for the education of children. The well-to-do family of

Niman Freedman, to whom Jewish learning was apparently of importance, hired a teacher for the instruction of the Freedman children exclusively. He spent a certain amount of time in private instruction with each child every weekday. He was given room and board in the house. On the Sabbath, when no business was transacted, it was the father's turn to take advantage of the teacher's services. In the best fashion of learned East European laymen, father and teacher rose at four o'clock on Saturday morning and studied Talmud together until eight. Then the children got up, they all had tea and started out for the synagogue.

This type of intensive study of Jewish subjects by all members of the family was, of course, the exception in the North End. There were many who could not afford or did not find it necessary to send their children even to *cheder*. In order to give at least some very basic instruction to their offspring, many of these became customers of the "*Siddur*-peddler." This was an itinerant teacher who from time to time knocked at the door of his student's home with a *Siddur* in his hand — hence the name — and gave the reluctant youngster a half hour's instruction in Hebrew reading. He collected a nickel or a dime for his services.

Preparation for the Bar Mitzvah was an important aspect of Jewish education.[43] In Europe, at that time, it rarely constituted a separate entity in the educational activity of the Jews. By following the ordinary process of schooling, the child automatically acquired most of the skills needed for participation in his own Bar Mitzvah. In America, however, many parents had neglected the teaching of their youngsters in their early years until they suddenly noticed that their boy was about "to become a man" and he was far from capable of acting as the *Maftir* in the hearing of the entire sacred assembly without bringing embarrassment to his relatives. As a result, a thriving Bar Mitzvah teaching activity began to be practiced by some teachers. The child would be taught practically nothing except to chant his portion in the service (without knowing the meaning of its content) and to recite his "speech" in Yiddish or in English (sometimes in Hebrew). As it happens too often in our own day, the little celebrant would call forth tears from the eyes of his elders by his fluent singing and by his oration drilled for many months even though he would be at a complete loss had he been given the task of reading any other portion of the Bible but his own.

The educational process rarely continued after the Bar Mitzvah age. Sometimes a child would be sent even after the Bar Mitzvah to see his *rebbe*, usually for the purpose of making sure that he put on his phylactaries and said his prayers. In Europe, many parents would strive to further the instruction of their children long after the Bar Mitzvah age in the hope of being able to send them some day to one of the *yeshivas*. In a few years, their son would return to the small town as a *talmid chochom* to the pride of his parents. To the majority who remained at home, the prestige of education in the society of the *shtetl* provided a powerful motivation for further learning. Nothing of the sort existed in the new world. Very soon after immigration, the acquisition of an American education became the ambition of young people and the dream of their parents. "The people who sat all day in the Chevra Shas wanted to make lawyers and doctors out of their boys and did nothing to give them at the same time a Jewish education" says one of the former North End residents.

No doubt, there were important economic considerations in such aspirations. The immigrants knew that their children would be spared the feeling of foreignness and the hard lot of peddlers and laborers only through the fruits of knowledge grown on native soil.[44] Yet one is inclined to believe that, beyond these practical considerations, the adoration for learning in itself, which had been part of the fabric of the Jewish mentality for many centuries, was responsible for the readiness with which parents made their children take advantage of the opportunities of learning which America offered them.

It is, therefore, understandable that all parents sent their children to the public schools — despite the many problems that this created from the standpoint of Jewish upbringing. The very idea of Jewish children constantly being in the company of gentile playmates could cause consternation to many immigrant parents. Indeed, in some areas in Europe, Jews had refused — partly for this reason — to comply with local laws making secular education compulsory for all children. Those of the Second-World-War Jewish immigrants whose orthodoxy is comparable to that of the immigrants of the eighties and nineties send their children today (with very few exceptions) to Hebrew-English all day schools. Here all English subjects are taught in a Jewish environment, thus giving an opportunity "for cultural integration without ethnic disintegration." The small minority of immigrant children in these schools becomes Americanized through English instruction and through contact with the third-generation majority. No such schools, of course, existed in the North End. The immigrants, therefore, sent their children to the public schools, making

59

awkward attempts to grant them Jewish knowledge in *chadorim* or by private tutors. One North Ender recalls: "The English school for the area was the Eliot School. In 1906, out of 54 graduates, about two-thirds were Jewish."

In a different interview:

Q. Tell me, was the Eliot School a high school too?

A. No, it was only a grammar school.

Q. Did all Jewish children go to that grammar school?

A. Yes, all.

Q. In other words, there was no tendency to keep the children home and teach them only Hebrew?

A. Oh, no! In addition to that we had a Hebrew school.

Attending high school was less popular among the North End Jews. Graduating from Eliot School (for boys) and from John Hancock School (for girls) was to most immigrant children the end of education. While all immigrants agreed on the necessity of public school education, the recognition of a need for high school studies, and especially for college attendance, was far from universal, particularly in the case of girls. One must not forget that at that time far fewer Americans in general went to high school or college, especially in the middle and lower income classes.

Q. What public school did they go to?

A. Hancock School for girls. But they went there only for [grammar] school. They did not believe in high school education for girls. They thought the girls would become too free.

Q. Did any girl go to college?

A. None that I know of. College was not necessary for girls in those days. They just had to learn how to cook.

The economic situation among the immigrants has to be kept in mind in this connection. Schooling was expensive. Furthermore, by the time children graduated from grammar school they were old enough to render much-needed help in the store or on peddling trips. If the young man went to school, this help was not forthcoming. "Not many families could spare even a minimal levy upon their budget for this purpose or, more crucial, the loss of earnings when youngsters were thus made unproductive."[45] One interviewee says: "Everyone who could possibly make it, tried to get into college. There was a general desire for learning. Of course, it was an expensive program and not everyone could afford it." To those, however, who could afford it, high school and even college represented an opportunity welcomed by parents and students alike:

Q. What was your father's attitude to such things as the children going to high school?

A. He insisted upon it. He wanted his children to have a very thorough English education.

Q. Did the rest of the Jews in the North End, your friends and neighbors, have the same attitude or did you consider this exceptional?

A. No. Not too many in those days went to college.

In a different interview:

Q. What do you think was the major factor in inspiring young people to go to college?

A. I think it was the fact that my father — and for that matter everyone I knew — regarded all intellectual pursuits as important. Desire for learning was a general attitude among the Jewish immigrants in those days. My father saw to it that all his children went to college. He himself wanted to learn.

Becoming acquainted with the culture of the new land was a quickly recognized necessity, which served very definite practical ends. Some of the immigrants, however, had misgivings — as this excerpt shows:

Q. What was the attitude of the older folks toward their children going to college?

A. Some of them did not mind. But in some, there was a fear that college would make them atheists.

Q. For those who did not go to college, was it this fear that prevented them?

A. No. Most of them did not go for economic reasons. Their parents could not pay for them and as soon as the boys were big enough to work, it was very important that they did their share. So that's why only a few of the boys went. But there was this case of [name omitted] who went to Harvard, then abroad to get his Ph.D., and married a gentile girl. His mother said, "To me, he is dead."

IN SUMMARY: the North End Jews attempted to bring up their children as well-integrated Americans who would be able to take full advantage of the opportunities present in the free society of America. They were anxious, therefore, to grant their children a good secular English education which they regarded as an instrument of both social integration and economic advancement. To this end, they took advantage of public educational facilities. They also attempted to imbue their children with a loyalty to Jewish values. However, the Jewish educational facilities available at the time were inadequate, old fashioned and totally unsuited to the American environment. Even more important was the changed attitude toward schooling as a result of which Jewish scholarship had lost its prestige-giving function to English education. The Jewish knowledge the first generation managed to impart to the second was consequently sketchy and superficial. This fact, however, caused the first generation immigrants much less agony than it would have caused the same kind of people in Europe. They felt rewarded — with or without justification — by the strides their children made in mastering the language and culture of the new land. The parents were tolerant towards the deviation from religious practice displayed by their growing children, and only in extreme cases was their resistance called forth. This attitude was partly responsible for the rather quick breakdown in observance by the second generation, demonstrated by a rapid spread of Sabbath-desecration and an extensive neglect of worship.

It is widely recognized that the second generation of most immigrant groups attempted to remove from themselves all vestiges of foreignness — "They tried to forget."[46] This tendency is, however, usually described as a "reaction," an attempt to "break away" from the old world ways of the first generation. The manner in which the North End immigrants went about bringing up their children seems to indicate that the second-generation's rapid acculturation was in fact of the making of the fathers.[47] By the profoundly changed attitudes of the immigrants, which their children were quick to discover despire tenacious external traditionalism, they helped shape the generation that marched headlong towards full Americanization.

7

summary and conclusions

SOME OF THE HISTORICAL and sociological conclusions based on the preceding material may be summarized as follows:

(1) The North End was the first exclusively Eastern European Jewish community established in the nineteenth century in the city of Boston. The first families moved there in the late 1860's and early 1870's.[48] With few exceptions, they came from the Russian Empire — most of them from Lithuania.

(2) Cheap housing, the closeness of the waterfront, the proximity of the Hanover Street business district and of the neighborhoods where many Irish and Italian customers of the Jewish peddlers lived, may have been some of the factors that made the Salem Street area suitable for the settling of these immigrants. In addition, it is possible that Eastern European Jews found it more pleasant to settle in a neighborhood not quite so close to that of their German co-religionists whose attitude to them was not always favorable.

(3) Up to the 1890's, the community constituted a mi-

nority in the area, scattered as they were among the gentile inhabitants. It became an overwhelmingly Jewish neighborhood only around and after the turn of the century.

(4) The social patterns of the smaller earlier group from the late sixties to the late nineties differed from those of the later community of immigrant masses. The early community was sociologically similar to the communities of the mid-century German Jewish immigrants. Peddling was, for example, more widespread than industrial employment. A tendency to relax observance was noticeable despite the strong Eastern European religious background of most immigrants. Linguistic acculturation was rapid. The financial conditions — after the first years — were regarded satisfactory by many people of the first generation, despite the rigors of the working conditions of the times. The later community had much more of the pressure, the poverty, the crowdedness and the turmoil typical of the urban areas of large scale immigrant settlement.[49] During this later period Jewish religious and cultural life experienced an upturn, which did not last long because many immigrants left the area after the first few years and the centers of Jewish community life were soon removed to other parts of the city and to the suburbs. Thus, while to most of the earlier inhabitants the North End was a place of more or less permanent settlement, to the later masses it was more of a temporary station.

(5) The people of the early community were enthusiastic about the freedom found in the new land. ("My father loved America. He hated like the dickens the idea of being a foreign born person.")[50] The aggressiveness they

displayed in winning for themselves an economic foot-
hold was perhaps one of the expressions of their con-
fidence in a good future in the land of their choosing.

(6) The atmosphere of freedom and the greater opportunities and burdens of making a living brought about
various social changes. One was a rising materialism in
Jewish society. The *amhoretz*, the person who had little
learning, became emancipated in a milieu in which the
task of making a living was paramount while education
was de-emphasized. The *apikoires* ("heretic"), who fought
an uphill battle in the *shtetl* against traditional beliefs,
had a much better chance in the less rigid American
Jewish environment. While excesses in overt irreligious
behavior were still condemned, the pressure against un-
orthodox pronouncements was much milder. Another
aspect was the change in the role of the members of the
family. The mother, for example, began to assume the
function of the person in charge of all educational and
synagogal matters. Growing children, helping in the
earning process, acquired a hitherto unknown status
within the family.

(7) There were two opposing tendencies in the first generation immigrants. In practice they were strictly observant and appeared to be guarding zealously the religious,
cultural and linguistic patterns of life which they brought
along with them from the old home. In their thinking,
however, they were prepared for changes in their way of
living, which they felt desirable under the new conditions. Thus, in theory, they leaned towards radical cultural changes even while they continued to live much as
they had in Europe. This attitude can be observed,
among other things, in the manner in which they

brought up their children. They were proud if they became "real Americans." They made sure they had a good English education. At the same time, they did not seem to be overly disturbed when the ethnically adverse effects of these aspirations became evident. The Bar Mitzvah teacher, the *Siddur*-peddler and even the *cheder* were ineffectual as agents of religio-cultural conservation. Parents were "understanding" and "lenient" when, as a result, their children abandoned important aspects of observance. The pride European Jewish parents took in the scholarship displayed by their children in the Hebrew subjects was gradually replaced by a clamor for English education. A synthesis of Judaism and Americanism seemed to them impossible. In their dilemma they tacitly decided in favor of the former for themselves and in favor of the latter for their children. Thus, their orthodoxy became superficial, resigned and inactive in contrast to the more ideology conscious, more aggressive orthodoxy of the twentieth century. The latter has addressed itself to the people of the second and third generations and its aim has been to show a way of Jewish traditional living on the American scene.

The members of the second generation, most of whom broke away completely from the ways of the first, were in reality only continuing on the path marked for them by their fathers. It seems to me that there are immigrant situations in which the decisive point in the process of cultural change is not in the second generation where the actual, visible adjustments are made but in the first, where the all-important attitudinal metamorphosis takes place. This idea, if correct, would lead us to concentrate in our studies of acculturation precisely on the phase in which overt adjustments are not yet observable. We may

An early North End cemetery.

A group of North End settlers pose for early cameraman sometime in the last quarter of 19th century

find that — barring perhaps quickly formed large enclaves — the characteristic mood of this phase is not a determined resistance to change but rather a reserved, but not at all reluctant, preparation for change.

(8) Another point that would perhaps warrant further study is the function of a "pilot" community in the social development of a Jewish neighborhood. When the large-scale immigration began, the newcomers found in the North End an established, well rooted Jewish community. Although small in numbers, the members of this community were the ones who gave the newcomers an example of American Jewish living. Residents who are described by interviewees as "prominent," "leading," or "influential" in the North End during the later period are usually found to have been members of the early families. They invariably seem to owe their prominence in the area to some activity related to aiding in the adjustment process of later immigrants. They were the experienced peddlers, many of them influential owners of peddlers' supply stores, bankers, manufacturers, community leaders — in short, people whose guidance the immigrants sought and needed. They, no doubt, had an important function in the acculturation of the later group. It could probably be demonstrated that, in general, if members of the same nationality arrive in successive waves of immigration, the later arrivals will not assimilate in the American environment directly. First, they will adjust to the already Americanized community of their own nationality. (In the case of the Jewish group, this may have had far-reaching consequences. The Jews were a people who, while in Europe, were native in various cultural environments. If a wave of Russian Jewish arrivals first assimilated to the earlier

69

German Jewish community, we may have the curious situation of Jews getting "Americanized" by acquiring patterns typical of the German-Jewish Americans only, not of Americans in general. Early Eastern European Jewish immigrants who have been under the influence of the German Jews may have further transmited these patterns to the later arrivals who also accepted them as the "American way.")

The Jews of Eastern European origin were destined to become in time the dominant element in the Boston Jewish community. Those fifty families who settled in the North End around and after 1870 set a pattern of adjustment for those who followed. Their avidity in commercial endeavor, their civic attitudes, their creeping religious liberalism, their fervor for American education were some of the ingredients of that pattern. By what was good and by what was bad in them, by what they did and by what they failed to do, they left their mark on the history of Boston Jewry.

notes

1. The general principles found in E. and N. Macoby, "The Interview: A Tool of Social Science" in G. Lindzey (ed.) *Handbook of Social Psychology* (Cambridge, Mass., 1954), and in Herbert Hyman *et. al.*, *Interviewing in Social Research* (Chicago, 1954), as well as in a number of articles in the *American Journal of Sociology* Vol. LXII No. 2 (September, 1956), were found helpful.

2. See Charles F. Cannell and Morris Axelrod, "The Respondent Reports on the Interview" in the *American Journal of Sociology* (September, 1956), p. 177.

3. "It is not easy to separate 'interview effects' from 'interviewer effects'" since "who tells what to whom under what conditions" is a basic problem in all social science interviewing. A favorable "homophilous" situation was created by the familiarity of the interviewer with the "world" the interviewees knew in their growing years. See M. Benney, D. Riesman, and S. A. Star, "Age and Sex in the Interview" in *American Journal of Sociology* (September, 1956), pp. 193-152; Herbert H. Hyman *et al.*, *op. cit.*, *passim*.

4. The more formal and technical problems arising from interviewing across language barriers are treated among others by Haim Blanc in "Multilingual Interviewing in Israel," in *American Journal of Sociology* (September, 1956), pp. 205-209.

5. "The North End is less than half a mile in any of its dimensions. It is a 'tight little island', hemmed in by continuous and ever-encroaching currents of commercial activity . . . The station thoroughfares lead to the markets, the markets extend to the docks. The docks reach around from the markets to the railroads again . . . . The interior form of the North End is that of one main highway to the East Boston Ferry, with a tributary street running on either side of it. The thoroughfare, Hanover Street, is cosmopolitan. Salem Street, toward the water, selected as a place of peaceful abode by Hebraist Puritans, is now, in the whirligig of time, turned over to the Hebrews themselves."
Robert A. Woods, *Americans in Process* (Boston, 1903), p. 2 quoted by Lee M. Friedman, *Pilgrims in a New Land* (Philadelphia, 1948), p. 438.

6. Interviewees disagree on the question of the relative age of the Jewish communities in the North and West Ends. Most of them consider the North End community to be older; some think the two emerged simultaneously. The former are probably correct. The *Boston City Directory* lists North End Jewish congregations from 1875 on; West End synagogues appear much later.

7. Max Margolis and Alexander Marx, *A History of the Jewish People* (Philadelphia, 1927), p. 694.

8. "In the old world they had been men of their village or province, and known by that name . . . . And the first societies they formed as well as the first churches they tried to set up were along such village and regional lines. But American life was too fluid to permit the indefinite perpetuation of these local identities." Will Herberg, *Protestant-Catholic-Jew* (New York, 1955), p. 24.

9. Oscar Handlin, *Adventure in Freedom* (New York, 1954), p. 84.

10. Article "Hebrews," in Edwin M. Bacon, *Kings Dictionary of Boston* (Cambridge, Mass., 1883).
"Salem Street . . . where Hebrew signs appear on all sides . . .

and moujik faces and costumes abound amid the old homes of the Phipses and other grandies . . . " M. F. Sweetser in *King's How to See Boston* (Boston, 1895), p. 188.

11. See Albert I. Gordon, *Jews in Transition* (Minneapolis, 1949), p. 17.

12. Ismar Elbogen, *A Century of Jewish Life* (Philadelphia, 1946), p. 333. See "The Russian Jewish Nightmare" in A. L. Sachar, *A History of the Jews* (New York, 1955), pp. 309-322.

13. See Margolis-Marx, *op. cit.*, p. 607.

14. Oscar Handlin, *The Uprooted* (The Universal Library Edition), p. 145.

15. This was Congregation Beth Abraham according to Rabbi Zalman Yakov Friederman writing in *Ozar Yisrael* Vol. III, p. 7. The *Boston City Directory*, however, lists "Shomri Shabos" [*sic*] from 1875 on, while "Bath Abraham" [*sic*] appears only in 1879.

16. From an article by Annie Kropp Adelson in "S.E.G. News, Cherry Tree Edition" (mimeographed, Boston, 1954), published by the Saturday Evening Girls. The S.E.G. was a North End girls group which met on Saturday evenings in the North End Branch Library to listen to stories from great books. According to the above publication, "this group is still meeting though many of the 'girls' are now grandmothers." In the "S.E.G. News, Cherry Tree Edition" some of the members published their life stories.

17. The function of satisfactory economic adjustment in the assimilative process is dwelt upon by W. C. Smith in *Americans in the Making*, pp. 168-173.
" 'Where bread is, there is my country' explains the readiness with which the immigrants in the eighteenth century, as well as in the twentieth, became Americans."

18. Handlin, *op. cit.* vividly treats the entire complex of immigrant problems with constant reference to village background.

19. Handlin, *Adventure in Freedom*, pp. 55-56, 95-97.

"He lacked the training and the skill to become a frontiersman; the ax, the gun and the ability to live off the soil was alike strange to him." *Ibid.*, p. 56.

20. The circumstances which made peddling in this period more difficult than earlier in the century are pointed out by Handlin, *op. cit.*, pp. 86-87.

21. See "Modern American Radanites" in Lee M. Friedman, *op. cit.*, p. 277 ff.

22. "Whenever they could do so, they would actually deny themselves food in order to be able to bring their relatives from abroad." Elbogen, p. 333.

23. Concerning the predicament of the intellectual immigrant, see W. C. Smith, *op. cit.*, p. 67. I feel that the loss of status by the intellectual was not only a result of the foreignness which the American saw in him and in the peasant equally. The disintegration of his own home society had robbed the intellectual of his privileged place and had challenged him in effect "to show how smart he is" in the changed circumstances where only practical accomplishments counted.

24. Rabbi Zalman Yakov Friederman in *Ozar Yisrael* (Hebrew) Vol. III., p. 8.

25. "Already the more prosperous Irish began to leave the North End and property value there was on the decline; it was then probably the lowest-valued real estate of the city. Rather naturally the poverty stricken incoming Jews began to fill the North End vacancies." Lee M. Friedman, *op. cit.*, p. 300.

26. About the architectural characteristics of the North End see *Kings Dictionary of Boston*, p. 323. About the activities of Jewish real estate men in the area and about the process of rebuilding the North End see Friedman, *op. cit.*, ch. 21, and the passages quoted there from the works of Robert A. Woods.

27. See Albert I. Gordon, *op. cit.*, pp. 193-195.

28. Barbara Miller Solomon, *Pioneers in Service* (Boston, 1956), p. 41.

29. See Gordon, p. 92.

30. "Immigrant women usually are more restricted and assimilate more slowly than men." W. C. Smith, *op. cit.*, p. 174. See note 24, the testimony of a North Ender.

31. See W. C. Smith, *op. cit.*, pp. 151-152; Handlin, *The Uprooted*, ch. 5.

32. See "The Immigrant As A Marginal Man" in W. C. Smith, *op. cit.*

33. "A person may hold opinions, attitudes, and sentiments which would be considered heretical by his group should he openly admit them. That, however, is impossible in the case of overt practices which others can observe." *Ibid*, p. 319.

34. *Boston Post*, April 16, 1901.

35. "East European Jewry came in two ideological streams. The great majority were religious Jews . . . A significant minority, however, had broken with Orthodoxy and with Jewish religion and were caught up in one or another of the secularist ideologies of the time, usually labor radicalism." Will Herberg, *Protestant-Catholic-Jew*, p. 193.

36. Banks were not always the large establishments the word today suggests. One North End "banker" for example sold delicatessen on the side on the premises of the "bank."

37. See note 15.

38. Robert A. Woods, *The City Wilderness* (Boston, 1898), p. 205, writes about the South End during this period: "Other Jewish associations hold religious services either in their own rooms or in halls hired for the purpose on the Jewish New Year and the Passover, if not oftener."

39. This Chevra Shas turned out to be one of the rather durable cultural institutions established in the North End. Repeatedly reorganized and expanded into a city-wide organization, it still meets every week for a Talmudic lecture given by Rabbi Dr. Joseph B. Soloveitchik, an international authority on Talmud

and Jewish philosophy. Today, however, lectures are in English and a large part of the participating group consists of second and third generation Jews. See Appendix 1.

40. See Handlin, *Adventure in Freedom*, p. 118; Zevi Scharfstein, *History of Jewish Education in Modern Times* (Hebrew; New York, 1947) Vol. 2, 177 ff.

40A. Miller Solomon, *op. cit.*, p. 18.

41. See Scharfstein, *op. cit.*, pp. 181-182.

42. For the adverse impression the cheder made on the Jewish child who compared it with his well-ordered public school, see, Hutching Hapgood, *The Spirit of the Ghetto* (New York, 1902), p. 23 ff.

43. See Albert I. Gordon, *Jews in Transition*, p. 126.

44. Herberg, *op. cit.*, pp. 21-22, points out that a rapid "deproletarianization" process set in immediately after the start of the short-term "proletarianization" of the Jewish masses following immigration. Thus, learning had some specific practical advantages which the immigrants were quick to recognize.

45. Handlin, *Adventure in Freedom*, p. 117.

46. Hansen, Marcus L., *The Problem of the Third Generation Immigrant*, Augustana Historical Society (Rock Island, Ill., 1937), quoted by Herberg, *op. cit.*, pp. 30 and 203; cf. p. 257.

47. "The assimilative forces which the dominant society exerts upon the ethnic groups are exerted primarily upon the child so that he, rather than the parent, becomes the transmitting agent of social change." Warner, W. Lloyd, *Structure of American Life* (Edinburgh, 1952), p. 126, quoted by Herberg, p. 37.

48. For the story of an 18th century Jewish resident in the North End see Lee M. Friedman, "Mr. Hays Speaks Out", *Menorah Journal*, Vol. XXVII, p. 77.

49. A slower pace in acculturation during this period was a result of this congestion: "At the North End the immigrant has remained foreign because isolation is possible there. His associates are his own countrymen. He does not become American for the simple reason that the North End is not American." Robert A. Woods, *The City Wilderness* (Boston, 1898), p. 38.

50. Another interviewee sums up the view prevalent among most immigrants: "To father it meant a place for hard work where you could get ahead quickly. It meant the possibility for progress, for a future, and for a career for his children."

glossary

Eastern European (Lithuanian) colloquial forms and pronunciation were followed in transcription.

AMHORETZ — A person ignorant in Jewish lore.

APIKOIRES — Disbeliever, "heretic."

BAAL KERIEH — Torah reader.

BALAGOLE — Driver of horse drawn carriage.

BAR-MITZVAH — Jewish male who reached "adulthood" by becoming 13 years old. Also: the celebration accompanying this event.

BILUIST — A member of the *Bilu* movement which advocated emigration from Europe to the Land of Israel.

CHADORIM — See *cheder.*

CHASSIDIM — Followers of the Chassidic movement founded in the 18th century by Rabbi Israel Baal Shem Tov.

CHAZN — Cantor.

CHEDER — A religious elementary school, usually privately conducted. Plural: *chadorim.*

CHEVRAH — A society.

CHUMESH — A book of the Pentateuch.

CHUPE — Wedding canopy.

GEMORE — Talmud.

IVRE — Hebrew Reading.

KAPOTE — Long black coat worn by Jews in Eastern Europe.

KAZATZKI — Fast Russian folk-dance.

KITL — White gown worn on High Holidays.

KOL NIDRE — First section of the Yom Kippur Eve service.

KREMER — Small storekeeper.

LANDSLEIT — See *landsmann.*

LANDSMANN — Countryman; emigrant from the same town. Plural: *landsleit.*

LANDSMANNSCHAFT — Organization of *landsleit.*

LITVAK — Lithuanian Jew.

MAFTIR — Person who reads the Prophetic portion after the conclusion of the Torah-reading.

MELAMED — Teacher. Plural: *melamdim.*

MINYAN — Quorum of ten adult Jewish males necessary for public religious service. Also: a religious service.

MOIHEL — Ritual circumciser.

REBBE — Teacher.

REBBE-GELT — Tuition.

RUSSISHE — Russian.

SFORIM — [Hebrew] books.

SHABES — Sabbath.

SHAMES — Beadle, sexton.

SHTETL — East European small town.

SHOICHET — Ritual slaughterer.

SHUL — Synagogue.

SIDDUR — Prayer book.

SIDRAH — Weekly Bible Portion

TALMID CHOCHOM — A person learned in Jewish lore.

TSHOLENT — A well known Sabbath dish.

UNTERFIRERS — Ushers who lead the groom and the bride to the wedding canopy.

YESHIVA — A school for Talmudic learning on a secondary or a higher level. In the United States also a Hebrew-English day school.

YOM KIPPUR — Day of Atonement.

appendices

A contemporary document and two newspaper articles are found in the three appendices on the following pages.

The first of these is the preamble to the by-laws of the Chevra Shas Hakelalith (General Talmudical Society) of Greater Boston. This organization grew out of the North End Chevra Shas when the latter was joined by groups of Talmud-students in other neighborhoods and established a city-wide Talmudical society. (See above Note 39). The Hebrew text reproduced and translated on the following pages is found in the society's ornate *Pinkes* (register) which was begun in 1913. In that year a scribe wrote the text by hand on the opening page of the *Pinkes* in beautiful square Hebrew characters, probably copying from the original document which was dated in the spring of 1882. It is not clear why the important paragraph before the last was copied in a manner differing from the rest of the text. The document closes with nineteen signatures, but it is not certain that all were affixed immediately at the time of the writing of the preamble.*

*The author is indebted to Rabbis Leo Abelow and Moses J. Cohen for permission to reproduce this preamble.

The document tells us much about what these North End talmudists thought of the situation of the Jew in the new country: their ideal to combine learning with business or a craft, their fear of material pursuits interfering with a healthy religious life and their determination to improve the prospects of Judaism in this country through increased learning.

The two articles from the Jewish Advocate were written by devoted North Enders who were deeply interested in the epic of their local community. They are reprinted here as an illustration for the methods, the interests and the types of data which are characteristic of early historiographic efforts made by faithful members of many local Jewish communities.

The critical historian can usually take advantage of the data assembled in such writings if he is aware of the profound emotional commitment of their authors. A deep adoration for the "pioneer Jews," pride in their accomplishments, and particularly in the successes of their well-Americanized descendants, gratitude to the country which made all this possible, interest in family relationships and in the appealing aspects of individual and community life are some of the basic attitudes in these writings. In the process of scientific historiography such materials must be evaluated with an understanding of the underlying attitudinal factors.

בעזהי״ת

יפה תלמוד תורה עם דרך ארץ 'שיגיעת שניהם משכחת עון 'וכל
תורה שאין עמה מלאכה סופה בטלה (אבות ב׳ משנה ב׳) אנחנו החֹם כאשר
נתאספנו יחד לטכֵס עצה ולהביט בעין חודרֵת על מצב היהדות ההרוסה
בארצות הברית בכלל ובעירינו באסטאן בפרט 'וכאשר ראו ראינו כי
אמנם ימצאו עוד יהודים נאמנים לה' ולתורתו אשר המה מן השרידים
המזהירים פה ושם לעבוד עבודת הקודש המסורה לכו מימי עולם
ומשנים קדמוניות, אך לדאבון לבנו בודדים הם במועדם וכל אחד
ואחד לדרכו פונה לרגל המלאכה ומלחמת החיים העמוסה עליהם אשר
עֹב כלנו כאיש אחד חברים הסכמנו בדעה אחת ליסד חברה שֹם ללמוד
בכל יום בחבורה גפֹת. למען החזק במעוֹז התורה ולחדש כנשר תחירֵת
האומה. וכל איש יהודי באשר הוא יהודי אחוז בחבלי בוז וקלֹסה בין
העמים אשר הוא שוכן בתוכם. יתעורר להתאחד בקבוץ ובדעה אחת
לבלי הרפות ידינו מהמפעל הנשגב הזה, ובכל מאמצי כחנו נשתדל לקבוע
שעה אחת מהשעות המתרגשות עלינו, וזכות התורה יעמוד לנו ולזרעֵנו
אחרינו להיות בתורת ה׳ חפצנו להגדיל תורה ולהאדירה. כי זה הוא היסוד
ואבן פנה לאושר בית ישראל לימים יוצרו, והבוחר בשערי ציון: שערים
המצוינים בהלכה; יברך את מפעלינו הטוב, ויזכנו ללמוד את התורה
מעושר ואושר, אמן עהֹה היום יום אֹף אמר תרמֹב לפֹק. מוסדות החברה יהי׳ עפֹ׳ התקנות המבוארות הלֹאה, ועֹז באנו

ואלו האנשים אשר נקבו בשמות אשר התנדבו לבם לקרבה ד אל
המלאכה מלאכת הקודש

אהרן בר הילל ארֹאנֹסֹאן	אברהם בהרב בֹר דוד
מרדכי בֹר שלמה קראנֹענֹבֹערֹג	מנחם מענדֹיל בֹר שאול
ברוך בֹר גבֹריאל גֹארֹדֹאן	אפרים בר יהושע הכהן
גבֹריאל משֹהבר ברוך גֹארֹדֹאן	אריה ליב בֹר יוסף יוזפֹא
אליעזר בהרב ר׳ מאיר חיים גֹודֹינֹסֹקי	שמואל ווילֹאֵנֹער
יצחק אליעזר קֹאהֹען	יוסף בר יצחק רֹיטֹצֹמֹאנֹד
שלמה שֹאפֹירֹא	מיכל בֹרֹדֹוב סלֹוצקֹי
שרגא איסר בהרב בֹר יוסֹף	יעקב אריה בֹר יצחק
אליעזר בֹר שמואל	אריה צבי גֹאלֹדֹבֹערֹג
יהודה בר יהושע הכהן	

I

Translation of Hebrew Document, Page 84

With the Help of God, Blessed Be He:

"An excellent thing is the study of the Torah combined with some worldly occupation, for the labor demanded by them both makes sin forgotten. All study of the Torah without work must in the end be futile." (Ethics of the Fathers [Chapter] 2, Mishnah 2.)

When we, the undersigned, assembled to take counsel and to observe with a penetrating eye the ruined condition of Judaism[1] in the United States in general and in our city of Boston in particular; and when we saw that one can indeed still find Jews faithful to the Lord and to his Torah — [people] who belong to the shining remnant [still extant] here and there — to carry out the holy work transmitted to them as a tradition from days of old and from former years; [and when we saw that] these [men] are, however, to the sorrow of our hearts, isolated in their stations and each one turns his own way according to [the limitations imposed by his] work and the battle of life which burdens [him]; we therefore agreed with one mind united as one man, to establish a Talmudical society to study the Talmud and its commentaries[2]

---

1. Lit. "the condition of ruined Judaism".

2. The expression rendered as "the Talmud and its commentaries" consists of the initial letters for Gemara, the commentary of Rashi, and Tosaphot.

every day in company in order to take hold of the pro-
tection of the Torah and to renew, as the eagle, the re-
vival of the nation. And every Jewish man — being a
Jew caught up in the cords of contempt and scorn
among the peoples in whose midst he dwells — shall
bestir himself to join [us] in one group and with one
mind so that they do not weaken our hands in this lofty
enterprise. And we shall attempt with the full exertion
of our power to set aside one hour of the [free] hours
that we may have and the merit of Torah shall stand by
us and by our descendants after us that our delight shall
be in the Law of the Lord, to magnify the Torah and to
glorify it. For this is the foundation and the cornerstone
of the happiness of the house of Israel for days to come.
He who has chosen the Gates of Zion, [which our sages
interpreted as] "the assemblies distinguished by the
study of the laws of Jewish life" — He shall grant us the
privilege to study Torah amidst prosperity and happiness.

The institutions of the society shall [function] according to the by-laws detailed further on. To this we affixed
our signature this Sunday of the weekly reading Emor
5642.[3]

These men who are mentioned by name are the ones
whose heart made them willing to come to do the work
— a work of holiness.

AARON, the son of Hillel, ARONSON
MORDECAI, the son of Solomon, KRONBERG
BARUCH, the son of Gabriel, GORDON
GABRIEL Moses, the son of Baruch, GORDON
ELIEZAR, the son of Rabbi Meir Hayim, GODINSKY
ISAAC ELIEZER KOHEN

3. The practice of dating documents by the day of the week and name
   of the Biblical portion to be read on the following Sabbath was widespread in Eastern Europe. The date corresponds to the 11th of Iyyar,
   April 30, 1882.

SOLOMON SHAPIRO
SHRAGA ISSAR, the son of Rabbi Joseph
ELIEZER, the son of Samuel
JUDAH, the son of Joshua HA-KOHEN
ABRAHAM, the son of David
MENAHEM MENDL, the son of Saul
EPHRAIM, the son of Joshua, HA-KOHEN
ARYEH LEIB, the son of Joseph, YOZPHA
SAMUEL WILLONER
JOSEPH, the son of Isaac, RICHMOND
MICHAL, the son of Dov, SLUTSKY
JACOB ARYEH, the son of Isaac
ARYEH ZEVI GOLDBERG

□□□□□□□□□□□□□□□□□□□□□□□□

II

Why a History of the North End?*

by Aaron Pinkney and Dr. Joseph I. Gorfinkle

"I had developed a burning desire to tell the story of the generation which cut its roots in the old home, crossed the ocean into a strange land and brought up its children to make their contribution to a free world. This would be the epitaph I should write upon the graves of those who had struggled heroically to open the gates of opportunity to me and to my children"

... From Prof. Morris R. Cohen's "A Dreamer's Autobiography."

Carlyle in his great classic, "Heroes and Hero Worship," states that history is made up of the biographies of great men. These men are the "salt of the earth," and a succession of accounts of their lives, their achievements and their influence upon their contemporaries, constitute the annals of the records of mankind.

History, however, as Professor Oscar Handlin of Harvard states, is not to be confined to the achievements only of "the respectably heroic individuals," so a history of the Jews of America should include "the struggle of the great mass of humble men and women who tried to carry across the ocean a tradition embodied in a way of life."

*Reprinted with permission from The Jewish Advocate, Passover Issue, 5710, Thursday, March 30, 1950.

Of late there is to be noted an awareness of the importance, in an account of Jewish life in America, of the Jewish communities as a whole, and not only of the scattered so-called great Jews of America.

What your and my grandfather and father accomplished is worthy of being noted and constitutes a matter of pride for us. Our parents and grandparents braved the stormy Atlantic, coming here with only their bare hands and ten fingers, yet see what they and their children have accomplished in a very, very short time! The success story of the Jewish immigrants is truly amazing.

Actuated by thoughts along these lines a group of men recently launched a movement to cast into permanent form the story of "The Jewish Pioneers of the North End of Boston *and their Descendants.*"

The first step in this project was taken two months ago when a group of men and women, descendants of North End Jewish immigrants, met at the home of Samuel Pinanski and most enthusiastically laid plans for the achievement of this objective. Those present were: Samuel Pinanski, chairman; Col. Bernard Gorfinkle, secretary; Mrs. Samuel Pinanski, Mrs. Jessie Berenson Barber, Aaron Pinkney, Dr. Joseph Brin, Ben G. Shapiro, Jack Krokyn, Max Levenson, Solomon Berenson, Harold Goldberg, Herman Dana, George Lourie, Edward S. Cantor and Ernest Dietz.

Mr. Pinanski was appointed chairman of a emporary committee; Colonel Bernard L. Gorfinkle, secretary; and Aaron Pinkney and Dr. Joseph I. Gorfinkle, historians. Since the meeting many prominent persons have assured the committee they will join the undertaking.

The Jewish Advocate advised the committee that in its publication will appear, at frequent intervals, "Stories of the Jews of North End."

The committee well realizes that there are some whose Americanism consists of denuding themselves of the culture and experiences of their ancestors, and others who have little desire for spending time or money in finding out about their antecedents.

Again, as is pointed out by C. R. Sherman in a Symposium recently conducted by YIVO on "Jewish Social Research in America," many of our organizations try with might and main to belittle Jewish otherness and make grotesque efforts to demonstrate what Jews are "not." They are "not" a race, "not" international bankers, "not" communities, do "not" control the press, do "not" own American industry, do "not" have much economic power in America and their political influence is "not" too great.

The North End project will serve to demonstrate as regards at least one small section of Jewry, what the Jews "have been," and "are," and what they have "done" and are "doing." *The influence of the pioneer Jews of the North End of Boston and their descendants has not been confined to Boston and New England alone, but has had national and even international importance.*

The need for such research and publication has been voiced by a number of competent authorities.

Lee M. Friedman, president of the American Jewish Historical Society, in a recent article entitled "The Significance of American Jewish History" calls for "the proper and truthful presentation and evaluation of the role which the Jew has played in the American scene, the study of his participation in shaping America, his con-

91

tribution to and share in the social, economic, political and intellectual life as an American and the tracing of his influence in shaping present conditions." This is our task and at the same time to present "the true picture of the struggle for group survival to preserve for American Jews their Judaism and Jewishness as an added enrichment of individual life."

Dr. A. S. Rosenbach, recent president of the American Jewish Historical Society, writes about the dream to be fulfilled of producing a history of the Jews in America from the discovery to the present day. He says, apropos of such a project that is now being undertaken: "Not only must we collect material in a systematic manner of the past, but it is necessary to marshal the records of our own time, of our own day, which will be invaluable in the years to come and will prove just as interesting to the reader of the future as the exploration, the colonial or the revolutionary period is to us today."

It is indisputable that there exists a need for the systematic and objective study of Jewish life in America. The "Pioneer Project" will concern itself with the past one hundred years of the development of North End Jewry and its outgrowths, which may be divided into four periods.

First period, 1850-1880: The early Jewish pioneers first settled in the North End. Some of them removed to the West End, East Boston and Chelsea, being the first settlers in these places, but the North End remained their synagogal, fraternal and social center.

Second period, 1880-1900: During these years the North End was at its peak of Jewish population, which grew greatly and rapidly, because of the influx of new immigrants. The original settlers began moving to

Somerville, Malden, Lowell, Worcester, Nashua and Manchester, N. H., Providence, R. I., to other New England cities and towns and to other parts of the country. This period was marked by the establishment of charitable, educational and fraternal organizations for the general community. Until 1890 the North End remained the center of the surrounding communities. Commerical enterprises developed rapidly during this period. The early pioneer settlers began giving way to the second generation.

Third period, 1900-1925: The leaders of the pioneer families who had come from the North End to the above mentioned centers established there all the communal activities. Shortly before the turn of the century, from these communities there began another trend of their residents to the lower Roxbury section, near Worcester Square, and what is now the Dudley Street Terminal. In 1900 a number of the early pioneer families of the North End located in the Blue Hill Avenue, Grove Hall, section of Roxbury, which subsequently developed into the largest Jewish settlement in New England, later extending into Dorchester, Mattapan and now reaching into Milton.

About 1925, many original North Enders continued their trek into Brookline and Newton, with similar results as to community leadership. Beginning in this period and extending to 1950 there came *the great development of the establishment of all the leading institutions, hospitals, homes for the aged and religious, charitable and educational agencies in which North Enders participated prominently. There was a continual growth of commercial enterprises.*

The youth of the third and fourth generations of the

pioneer settlers completed their educational careers, entering professional and business life, marrying and raising families of the fifth and sixth generations of North Enders.

Fourth Period, 1925-1950: During this last period, which brings us to the close of a century of important Jewish development beginning in the old North End section of Boston, and where at the present time there is not one Jewish family residing, we find many descendants of this Jewry prominent in every walk of life, not only in Boston and in New England, but throughout the country. In the arts and sciences, in literature and the professions, in drama, music and commercial enterprises, they have made outstanding contributions and achieved great successes. They are among leaders in all communal endeavors and their names and careers are recorded in many "Who's Who" publications.

Moreover, now is the time to set down these achievements. With the cessation of immigration in 1914, the Jewish communities have attained a great deal of stability so that it is not a difficult task to chronicle the necessary facts. There has been no destruction of data as in Europe and basic records are easily found at hand.

It remains only for the "North Enders" to devote time, money and some energy to perpetuate the deeds of the past which will be an inspiration and an incentive to our contemporaries and our children to continue on the same high plane of civic, cultural, religious and philanthropic endeavor, so that their descendants may rise up in turn and call them blessed.

III

Do You Know of the Old North End?*

By AARON PINKNEY

MOSES MICHAEL HAYS, a Grand Master of Masons of Massachusetts during Colonial days, and his family were the first Jews to live in the North End. Their residence was at Hanover Street. Hays introduced the Scottish Rite of Masonry in this country. Paul Revere was Deputy under him. Hays' nephews, Judah and Abraham Touro, in their younger days lived with him.

ONE OF THE FIRST POLISH JEWS to settle in Boston, one hundred years ago, was Joseph Wyzanski. From the Wyzanski family, their relatives and landsleit came most of the pioneer Jewish settlers in the North End.

ABOUT THE YEAR 1880 the North End Jews began to displace the German Jews as the dominating element in Boston. Today their children and grandchildren can be found among the leaders in all community activities.

FROM THE PIONEER NORTH END FAMILIES came the following leaders of Temples and Congregations: Temple Ohabei Shalom, now in its 107th year, Henry Penn, president. Temple Israel, the following trustees: Max E.

Reprinted, with permission, from the Jewish Advocate, September 22, 1949.

95

Wyzanski, Judge Abraham E. Pinanski, Abraham C. Webber, John S. Slater, Sidney R. Rabb. Temple Mishkan Tefila, Joseph Wyzanski was one of the first presidents when this temple was at Ash Street, Abraham Bloom, honorary president, Meyer H. Slobodkin, vice-president. At Congregation Kehillath Israel, Brookline, the founders were North Enders. At one time Joseph Rudnick was president; Simon Hirshberg, vice-president; Selig Lipsky, treasurer; Harry Edelsteine, trustee. Joseph Rabinovitz, treasurer for 25 years, now succeeded by his brother, Jacob Rabinovitz. Hyman M. Hillson was first president of Temple B'nai B'rith, Somerville. Judge Abraham E. Pinanski is director of Congregation Adath Jeshurun, Roxbury, which his father founded along with Louis Shain, a recent president of this Congregation. At the Congregation in Miami, Florida, Harry Magid was one of the first presidents.

NORTH ENDERS were leaders in establishing the Beth Israel and Jewish Memorial Hospitals, Benoth Israel Sheltering Home, Home for Aged, Children's Home, Immigrant Aid Society, Free Loan Society, Free Burial Society, Moeth Hitem, Greater Boston Fuel and Aid Society and other beneficial societies.

THREE OF THE FIVE PRESIDENTS of the Beth Israel Hospital, [Boston,] were North Enders: Abraham Ginzberg, David Watchmaker and Casper Grosberg. David Gould is president of the Jewish Memorial Hospital. Dr. Maurice Gerstein and Dr. Simon Richmond were Physicians-in-Chief of this hospital and Dr. Harry Linenthal, for many years Physician-in-Chief at the Beth Israel Hospital, and Dr. Samuel A. Levine, world renowned heart specialist who recently was the second American ever to be invited to deliver the annual St. Cyres lecture before the Royal Society of Medicine, at London, England, are North Enders.

LOUIS KRONBERG, world renowned artist; Bernard Berenson, renowned art critic; Prof. Horace Kallen; Prof. Bernard Richards; Rabbi Joseph I. Gorfinkle, all renowned authors, are North Enders.

WILLIAM I. WYMAN (Isaac Wyzanski) was born at Stillman Street, North End, graduated from M.I.T. as a naval architect, reconditioned Admiral Dewey's battleship during the Spanish American War; later entered the U. S. Patent Department and was mentioned in an article in the Saturday Evening Post as the great authority of that department.

HARRY D. WHITE, Assistant Secretary of the U. S. Treasury, Professor of Economics at Harvard, author of the Bretton Woods World Monetary Plan, President Roosevelt's and Henry Morgenthau's advisor on finances, was a North Ender.

THE HON. JUSTICES, the late David A. Lourie, Abraham E. Pinanski, Lewis Goldberg, of the Massachusetts Superior Court; Philip Rubenstein, Israel Ruby and Niman Kolodny of Massachusetts Courts; and Max L. Pinanski of Maine Bench, are North Enders.

HON. ARTHUR REINHART (Reinherz), recently elected a State Senator of New Hampshire, first Jew to hold that office in that state, is from one of the pioneer Jewish families of the North End.

THE LATE HON. ABRAHAM C. RATSHESKY, a United States Ambassador to Czechoslovakia, and his father,

Asher, who was the first Jew to build commercial buildings on Hanover Street, North End, 1875-82, conducted their large retail clothing business there until they went into banking.

RETAIL CLOTHING MERCHANTS Leopold Morse, Simon Vorenberg, Nathan Waxman, Simon Bernard, Bernard M. Wolf, and in other men's lines the Hermansons, Isaacsons, Wingerskys and Raphaels all had their retail stores in the North End.

ISAAC PINKOFSKY was the first Jew to be elected to the Chelsea, [Mass.,] City Council, 1887-88. His parents were among the first Jews to settle in East Boston and Chelsea in the early '70s and '80s and were from the North End.

THE FIRST MILITARY COMPANY made up entirely of Jewish men, became part of the Massachusetts Militia during the Spanish-American war. They were all North Enders. It was organized by Samuel H. Borofsky, who was its Captain. Abraham Moss was a Civil War veteran. Col. Bernard L. Gorfinkle won marked distinction in the first World War. Joseph Wilner (Wyzanski) served in the Spanish-American, First and Second World Wars.

NORTH ENDERS FOUNDED two of the first Zionist organizations in this country. In 1891 the B'nai Zion Educational Society and the Chova Zion. Jacob Askowith and his son Dr. Charles Askowith designed the Zion Flag, which for the first time was carried in a public parade in 1892 in Boston. Isaac Harris, a member, was one of the first delegates to the first Zionist Congress at Bazle, Switzerland. The famous Jewish poet, Imber, author of Hatikvah, made his headquarters at the B'nai Zion Hall in the North End when in Boston.

SAMUEL KRONBERG, a noted singer, music teacher and grand opera producer, who managed the famous singer, Madam Tetrizina and Composer Mascagni in his tour in this country, was one of the pioneers of the North End and was the first president of the Benoth Israel Sheltering Home.

BARNARD GINSBERG was one of the earliest pioneers of the North End. He was a brother-in-law by his first wife of Samuel and Louis Kronberg, whose daughter by his second wife is the wife of Jesse Laskey, of moving picture fame.

MORRIS GEST, famous theatrical producer, came to Boston with a tag pinned to his coat addressed to Freedman Brothers, Salem Street, where he received his first employment in their peddlers' supply store.

THE FAMOUS ACTRESS, Sophie Tucker, as a child, and her parents lived at 22 Salem Street and went to the Cushman School at Parmenter Street. Her first appearance as an actress was at the Howard Atheneum, North End.

A LARGE NUMBER OF NORTH ENDERS have made outstanding successes in commercial enterprises. To mention a few: the Rabinovitz (Rabb) family in large chain grocery [retailing,] their father and grandfather who, in 1891, opened a grocery store at Salem and Prince Streets, in the North End. Samuel Magid started his novelty jewelry business at Cross Street, North End, moved to Providence, R. I., became one of the leading manufacturers of novelty jewelry in the country and was one of the first Jews to build a hotel at Miami Beach, Florida. The Tichnor Brothers, leading postcard manufacturers, started their business near Cross Street. Tichnor Bros. and Samuel Magid were mentioned in The Saturday Evening Post special articles dealing with their [enterprises.] The Sandlers, shoe manufacturers, [established a] retail store at Cross Street which has been owned by this family since 1892. Barron, Anderson Company, leaders in overcoat manufacturing; the Agoos, Kaplan, Goldman, Gordon families in leather; the Axelrod family in fabrics; the Alberts, Sonnabend, Fish and Goldstein families in jewelry [all have their roots in the North End.]